AN ASSESSMENT OF RULES OF ORIGIN IN RCEP AND ASEAN+1 FREE TRADE AGREEMENTS

Pramila Crivelli, Stefano Inama, and Mark Pearson

OCTOBER 2023

ASIAN DEVELOPMENT BANK

Contents

Tables, Figures, and Boxes

Tables

Figures

Boxes

Abbreviations

AANZA	ASEAN-Australia-New Zealand Free Trade Agreement
ADB	Asian Development Bank
ACFTA	ASEAN-People's Republic of China Free Trade Agreement
AJCEP	ASEAN-Japan Comprehensive Economic Partnership
AKFTA	ASEAN-Republic of Korea Free Trade Agreement
ASEAN	Association of Southeast Asian Nations
ATIGA	ASEAN Trade in Goods Agreement
CC	Change of Chapter
CO	Certificate of Origin
CPTPP	Comprehensive and Progressive Agreement for Trans-Pacific Partnership
CTC	Change of Tariff Classification
CTH	Change of Tariff Heading
CTSH	Change of Tariff Subheading
FOB	Freight on Board
FTA	Free Trade Agreement
HS	Harmonized System
PSRO	Product-Specific Rules of Origin
RCEP	Regional Comprehensive Economic Partnership
RVC	Regional Value Content
US	United States
VNM	Value of Non-Originating Materials
VOM	Value of Originating Materials
WO	Wholly Obtained

Acknowledgments

This report was prepared by the Regional Cooperation and Integration Division (ERCI) of the Economic Research and Development Impact (ERDI) of Asian Development Bank (ADB). It was supported by the ADB technical assistance project, TA 6740: Raising the Value of Regional Trade Agreements—Key Factors for Successful Implementation and Positive Economic Impact, financed by ADB's Technical Assistance Special Fund and the Regional Cooperation and Integration Fund. The authors are Pramila Crivelli, ERCI economist; Stefano Inama, chief at the United Nations Conference on Trade and Development; and Mark Pearson, ADB consultant. Paulo Rodelio Halili and Pramila Crivelli coordinated the production of this report under the supervision of Jong Woo Kang, director, ERCI. Jeremy Marand, ADB consultant, provided data and editorial assistance.

Eric Van Zant edited the manuscript, and Michael Cortes created the cover design and implemented the typesetting and layout. Jess Alfonso Macasaet proofread the report, while Levi Lusterio handled the page proof checking, with support from Paulo Rodelio Halili. The Printing Services Unit of ADB's Corporate Services Department and the Publishing Team of the Department of Communications and Knowledge Management supported printing and publishing.

1. Introduction

One of the most quoted advantages of the Regional Comprehensive Economic Partnership (RCEP) is its provision of a common rules of origin platform addressing the "noodle bowl" effect of overlapping free trade agreements (FTAs) in Asia and the Pacific. Each Association of Southeast Asian Nations plus-1 (ASEAN+1) free trade agreement (FTA)[1] has a different set of rules of origin and operational certification procedures generating compliance costs for firms.

From this perspective, the RCEP looks like a troubleshooter, providing opportunities to simplify the current rules of origin tangle in Asia. Yet the Asian Development Bank (ADB) study—An Analysis of the Product-Specific Rules of Origin of the Regional Comprehensive Economic Partnership[2]—found that the product-specific rules of origin of the RCEP are not the most liberal compared to those of ASEAN Trade in Goods Agreement (ATIGA) and the Comprehensive and Progressive Agreement for Trans-Pacific Partnership (CPTPP). The study also shows that the cumulation facilities contained in the RCEP, perceived as a distinct advantage of RCEP over other FTAs given its wide membership, are, in practice, difficult to use due to the tariff differentials and the incomplete status of the cumulation provisions.[3]

ASEAN member states have entered a series of FTAs with several RCEP partners. A number of concurrent factors are crucial in determining how the potential RCEP advantages can be turned into concrete trading opportunities for firms aiming to use the RCEP over and above the existing tangle of FTAs. First, it needs to be assessed whether the RCEP provides any incremental market access in terms of tariff preferences and rules of origin over the existing ASEAN+1 FTAs.

The preferential margin[4] offered to firm when using the RCEP instead of existing ASEAN+1 FTAs is one of the most critical factors affecting ASEAN firms' incentives to trade among themselves using the RCEP.

---

[1] ASEAN+1 FTAs are agreements establishing free trade areas between ASEAN member economies as a group and individual non-ASEAN dialogue partners, including Australia and New Zealand, the People's Republic of China, India, Japan, the Republic of Korea, and Hong Kong, China.

[2] See Asian Development Bank (ADB). 2022. *An Analysis of the Product-Specific Rules of Origin of the Regional Comprehensive Economic Partnership.* http://dx.doi.org/10.22617/TCS220167-2.

[3] The extent and scope of cumulation at the entry into force of the RCEP is limited to cumulation of originating materials. The cumulation of working or processing within the RCEP is going to be discussed at a later stage during the implementation of the RCEP built-in agenda. See paragraph 2 of Article 3.4 of the RCEP rules of origin in Regional Comprehensive Economic Partnership Agreement (RCEP). 2020. Legal texts. https://rcepsec.org/legal-text/. 2. "The Parties shall commence a review of this Article on the date of entry into force of this Agreement for all signatory States. This review will consider the extension of the application of cumulation in paragraph 1 to all production undertaken and value added to a good within the Parties. The Parties shall conclude the review within five years of the date of its commencement, unless the Parties agree otherwise". See also https://blogs.adb.org/blog/making-rcep-successful-through-business-friendly-rules-origin.

[4] The preferential margin is the difference from the normal rates of duty (most-favored nation) and the preferential tariffs granted to FTA partners.

Detailed analysis has not been carried out comparing the tariff preferences available under ASEAN+1 FTAs and the RCEP. However, given that (i) tariff dismantling under the ASEAN+1 FTAs has been completed and (ii) research[5] has established that the RCEP tariff phase out schedules are long and complicated, the RCEP, for many years to come, may not necessarily offer better preferential tariffs than those available under existing ASEAN+1 FTAs.

This study thus complements the findings of the previous ADB publication, providing a comparative assessment of the RCEP product-specific rules of origin (PSROs) with those contained in ASEAN+1 FTAs. This comparative assessment is carried out on the leniency and stringency of PSROs in terms of manufacturing requirements and whenever possible the scope of convergence among these FTAs.

---

[5]   For the tariff offers under the RCEP, see their complex structure and the tariff differential rules that may affect the day-to-day implementation of cumulation in Pramila Crivelli and Stefano Inama. 2022. A Preliminary Assessment of the Regional Comprehensive Economic Partnership. *ADB Briefs*. No. 206. http://dx.doi.org/10.22617/BRF220009-2.

ATIGA rules of origin and their various iterations influenced the design of those rules in the ASEAN+1 FTAs. During negotiations with ASEAN+1 partners, ASEAN economies and their partners are known to have different views on the desirable model of rules of origin as a basis for the negotiations. These contrasting negotiating positions have contributed to a multitude of different PSROs and associated operational certification procedures currently applied under ASEAN+1 FTAs.

Recall that ASEAN rules of origin embedded in the latest formulation of ATIGA of 2009 are themselves the result of an extremely long history of iterations dating from the ASEAN Free Trade Area of 1992.[6] These, however, still contain numerous loopholes in terms of transparency and predictability.

Together with the CPTPP, the text of RCEP rules of origin is among the latest formulations of such rules in Asia and the Pacific. In spite of its milestone achievement, as shown in the earlier study, best practices and lessons learned are not well reflected into the RCEP rules of origin general provisions, PSROs, and operational certification procedures. Many key aspects are still left to the built-in agenda.

The RCEP shows a series of similarities with ATIGA and some of the ASEAN+1 FTAs. The RCEP also contains features reflecting the influence of different ways of drafting rules of origin inherited from the vast experience of Australia, Japan, and New Zealand.

One of the main ways RCEP differs from ATIGA and from the majority of ASEAN+1 FTAs is its pragmatic approach of adopting a complete annex of PSRO instead of general rules of origin (or regime-wide) applicable across the board. Initially the ASEAN-Australia New Zealand FTA (AANZA) followed the same structure of regime-wide rules of origin (the regional value content [RVC]40[7] or change of tariff heading [CTH]) coupled with a list of PSRO, partly to satisfy the ASEAN requests. Most recently, AANZA embraced the adoption of a full list of PSRO, abandoning the idea of general rules of origin, following what is now general practice.

As discussed in former studies,[8] the RCEP has also adopted a full list of PSROs applying almost verbatim the CPTPP text about the definition of main origin requirements. This marks a significant improvement of the RCEP over ATIGA and over the ASEAN-People's Republic of China Free Trade Agreement, ASEAN-Japan Comprehensive Economic Partnership Agreement, and the ASEAN-Republic of Korea Free Trade Agreement.

Thanks to this drafting improvement, the RCEP addresses the lack of clarity in ATIGA in the sequencing of application of general rules and PRSOs.

---

[6]   See Stefano Inama and Edmund Sim. 2015. *Rules of Origin in ASEAN: A Way Forward.* Cambridge: Cambridge University Press.

[7]   Regional value content of 40%.

[8]   See ADB. 2022. *An Analysis of the Product-Specific Rules of Origin of the Regional Comprehensive Economic Partnership.* http://dx.doi.org/10.22617/TCS220167-2.

Table 1 compares the main legal text concerning the architecture of main rules of origin criteria. The architecture of rules of origin is meant to be the sequencing of application of main criteria of rules of origin, i.e., (i) only product-specific rules of origin "PSRO Only" or (ii) "across the board" or "general/regime-wide" criteria to determine origin and an annex of PSRO, (iii) any combination of the above, and (iv) the sequencing of application among general rules and PSROs, where applicable.

Notably, in this context, both the RCEP and AANZA explicitly reference an annex containing PSROs and do not mention a general rule of origin.

In contrast, ACFTA, AJCEP, and AKFTA texts contain a formulation of a general rule of origin.

Yet there are significant variations of formulation of the general rules of origin among ACFTA, AJCEP, and AKFTA. In fact, AJCEP and AKFTA general rules of origin are based on an alternative between RVC 40 or CTH.

The ACFTA formulation differs from the practice in ATIGA, AJCEP, and AKFTA with a rather convoluted legal text[9] as shown in Table 1 (page 5), adopting a three-tier approach: (i) an RVC 40 requirement as main general rule, (ii) a CTH or RVC 40 requirement for a number of HS chapters (iii) an annex of product-specific rules contained in attachment that applies exclusively, i.e., there is no alternative general rule.

The sequencing of application and the drafting of Article 4 is not entirely clear as paragraph 1 of Article 4 of ACFTA shown in Table 1 makes an explicit carve out from the general rule of origin for the products contained under paragraph 2 "except for those goods covered under Paragraph 2." Normally such exclusion from the general rule means that the goods covered under paragraph 2 are subject to PSRO.

Yet, paragraph 2 of Article 4 is contradictory when it provides that "In accordance with Paragraph 1, and unless otherwise provided for in the Product-Specific Rules as specified in Attachment B a good shall be treated as an originating good if it meets a regional value content of not less than 40 per cent or those criteria in the Product-Specific Rules."

This confusing sentence seems to introduce a default RVC 40 alternative rule in addition to the PSRO requirements contained in attachment B.

The distinct architecture of the main rules of origin criteria in ACFTA, from other ASEAN+1 FTAs, and the RCEP has a sizeable impact on the counting of the convergence coding, as section 5 discusses.

---

[9]   According to insights from officials present during negotiations, the poor drafting was due to a lack of time reviewing the draft legal text before its presentation to ministers for formal adoption.

Table 1: Comparison of the Architecture of Rule of Origin Criteria in RCEP and ASEAN+1 FTAs

RCEP	AANZA	ACFTA	AJCEP	AKFTA
"**Article 3.2: Originating Goods.** For the purposes of this Agreement, a good shall be treated as an originating good if it is: (a) wholly obtained or produced in a Party as provided in Article 3.3 (Goods Wholly Obtained or Produced); (b) produced in a Party exclusively from originating materials from one or more of the Parties; or (c) produced in a Party using non-originating materials, provided the good satisfies the applicable requirements set out in Annex 3A (Product-Specific Rules), and meets all other applicable requirements of this Chapter."	"**Article 4: Goods Not Wholly Produced or Obtained** 1. For the purposes of Article 2.1(b) (Originating Goods), a good shall qualify as an originating good of a Party if it satisfies all applicable requirements of the Product-Specific Rules. 2. Where Annex 2 (Product-Specific Rules) provides a choice of rule between a regional value content based rule of origin, a change in tariff classification based rule of origin, a specific process of production, or a combination of any of these, a Party shall permit the producer or exporter of the good to decide which rule to use in determining if the good is an originating good."	"**Article 4 Goods Not Wholly Produced or Obtained** 1. For the purposes of Article 2(c) of this Annex, except for those goods covered under Paragraph 2, a good shall be treated as an originating good: (a) if the good has a regional value content of not less than 40 per cent of FOB calculated using the formula as described in Article 5 of this Annex, and the final process of production is performed within a Party; or (b) for the purpose of goods classified in Chapters 25, 26, 28, 29[b], 31[c], 39[d], 42–49, 57–59, 61, 62, 64, 66–71, 73–83, 86, 88, 91–97 of the Harmonized System if all non-originating materials used in the production of the goods have undergone a change in tariff classification (hereinafter referred to as "CTC) at the four-digit level, which is a change in tariff heading, of the Harmonized System. 2. In accordance with Paragraph 1, and unless otherwise provided for in the Product-Specific Rules as specified in Attachment B, a good shall be treated as an originating good if it meets a regional value content of not less than 40 per cent or those criteria in the Product-Specific Rules."	"**Article 26: Goods Not Wholly Obtained or Produced** 1. For the purposes of paragraph (b) of Article 24, a good shall qualify as an originating good of a Party if: (a) the good has a regional value content (hereinafter referred to as "RVC), calculated using the formula set out in Article 27, of not less than forty (40) per cent, and the final process of production has been performed in the Party; or (b) all non-originating materials used in the production of the good have undergone in the Party a change in tariff classification (hereinafter referred to as "CTC") at the 4-digit level (i.e., a change in tariff heading) of Harmonized System."	"**Rule 4: Not Wholly Obtained or Produced Goods** 1. For the purposes of paragraph 1(b) of Rule 2, a good, except those covered under Rule 5 as provided for in Appendix 2, shall be deemed to be originating if the regional value content (hereinafter referred to as the "RVC") is not less than 40% of the FOB value or if a good has undergone a change in tariff classification at four digit-level (change of tariff heading) of the Harmonized System."

AANZA FTA = ASEAN-Australia New Zealand FTA, ACFTA = ASEAN-People's Republic of China FTA, AJCEPA = ASEAN-Japan Comprehensive Economic Partnership Agreement, AKFTA = ASEAN-Korea Free Trade Agreement, CTC = change of tariff classification, FOB = freight on board, RCEP = Regional Comprehensive Economic Partnerhsip, RVC = regional value content.

[a]   See Annex 1 of Protocol to Amend the Framework Agreement on Comprehensive Economic Cooperation and Certain Agreements thereunder between the Association of Southeast Asian Nations (ASEAN) and the People's Republic of China. ASEAN-People's Republic of China (ACFTA). 2019. Legal texts. https://www.enterprisesg.gov.sg/-/media/esg/files/non-financial-assistance/for-companies/free-trade-agreements/ASEAN-China-FTA/upgrade-protocol/ANNEX-1-Rules-of-Origin.pdf.

[b]   "For Headings 29.01 and 29.02, the applied criterion is RVC 40 unless otherwise mutually agreed by the Parties."

[c]   "For Headings 31.05, the applied criterion is RVC 40, unless otherwise mutually agreed by the Parties."

[d]   "For Headings 39.01, 39.02, 39.03, 39.07 and 39.08, the applied criterion is RVC 40, unless otherwise mutually agreed by the Parties."

Source: Authors based on RCEP, AANZA, ACFTA, AJCEP, and AKFTA legal texts.

Table 2 compares the calculation methodology for rules of origin expressed using a regional value content (RVC) requirement. As discussed above, an RVC can be used as a general regime-wide rule of origin or as a PSRO.

Table 2: Comparison of Calculation Methodology in Determining Regional Value Content

Free Trade Agreement	Main Origin Criteria	Numerator/Denominator of Ad Valorem Percentage Criterion	Regime-Wide RVC Percentage	Method of Ad Valorem Percentage Calculation
AANZFTA	PSRO only[a]	*Direct method:* Value of originating materials (VOM) + cost of direct working or processing + profit Denominator: FOB price *Indirect method:* A subtraction from the FOB price of the value of non-originating materials (VNM)[b] Denominator: FOB price	Not less than 40%	*Direct method:* Value added calculation *Indirect method:* Subtraction of value of non-originating materials from the FOB price
ACFTA	RVC, RVC or CTC[c] at 4-digit level, i.e., CTH	*Direct method:* FOB price—VNM Denominator: FOB price	Not less than 40% according to the direct formula	*Direct method:* Based on a 40% of RVC requirement
AJCEP	RVC or CTC at 4-digit level, i.e., CTH	*Indirect method:* FOB price—VNM Denominator: FOB price	Not less than 40%	Subtraction of the VNM from the FOB price
AKFTA	RVC or CTC at 4-digit level, i.e., CTH	*Build-up method:* VOM Denominator: FOB price *Build-down method:* FOB price—VNM Denominator: FOB price	Not less than 40 per cent	*Build-up method:* Based on the VOM *Build-down method:* Based on the VNM
RCEP	PSRO only[d]	*Direct method:* VOM + cost of direct working or processing + profit Denominator: FOB price *Indirect method:* A subtraction from the FOB price of the VNM[e]Denominator: FOB price	No less than 40 per cent	*Direct/build-up method:* Value added calculation *Indirect/build-down method:* Subtraction of VNM from the FOB price

AANZA FTA = ASEAN-Australia New Zealand FTA, ACFTA = ASEAN-People's Republic of China FTA, AJCEPA = ASEAN-Japan Comprehensive Economic Partnership Agreement, AKFTA = ASEAN-Korea Free Trade Agreement, CTC = change in tariff classification, CTH = change of tariff heading, FOB = freight on board, PSRO = product-specific rules of origin, RCEP = Regional Comprehensive Economic Partnership, RVC = regional value content, VOM = value of originating materials, VNM = value of non-originating materials.

[a] From 1 January 2022, PSRO should be used in place of a change in tariff classification (CTC), change of tariff heading (CTH), regional value content (RVC), and otherwise qualifies as an originating good (OTH) in the Integrated Cargo System.

[b] The value of non-originating materials shall be for imported materials, the cost, insurance, and freight value of the materials at the time of importation; and for materials obtained within a party, the earliest ascertainable price paid or payable. A material of undermined origin shall be treated as a non-originating material.

[c] Non-originating materials used must have undergone a CTC at the 4-digit level of the HS code for goods classified in Chapters 25, 26, 28, 29, 31, 39, 42–49, 57–59, 61, 62, 64, 66–71, 73–83, 86, 88, 91–97*
*For Headings 29.01, 29.02, 31.05, 39.01, 39.02, 39.03, 39.07, and 39.08, the applied criterion is RVC40, unless otherwise mutually agreed by the Parties.

[d] Product-specific rules.

[e] The VNM shall be for imported materials, the cost, insurance, and freight value of the materials at the time of importation; and for materials obtained within a Party, the earliest ascertainable price paid or payable. A material of undermined origin shall be treated as a non-originating material.

Source: Authors based on RCEP, AANZA, ACFTA, AJCEP, and AKFTA legal texts.

As Table 2 shows, the RVC concept is common in Asian FTAs. Importantly, the concept of RVC embeds the notion of cumulation. In fact, the *ad valorem* percentage threshold will be met as a region or as parties to the same FTA and not as an individual country. This sounds like a trade facilitating approach, but in the case of mega-regionals like the RCEP, the RVC concept has to be confronted with the multiplicity of partners that may adopt different tariff offers in their schedules toward RCEP partners. This means that during the implementation phase of the tariff phase down, additional provisions have been inserted into the RCEP to allocate origin to one partner when two countries or more have been involved in the production of a good. These provisions are contained in the tariff differentials[10] embedded in the RCEP tariff offers.

The RVC calculations in RCEP and ASEAN+1 FTAs are similar, as shown in Table 2, but differences exist, mostly deriving from the heritage of ASEAN rules of origin and the different models Australia, the Republic of Korea, and New Zealand used in calculating RVC.

A first difference is contained in the wording: *Indirect method or direct method* used to refer to the methodology in most ASEAN+1 FTAs or *build-up or build down* in AKFTA.

The *direct or indirect method* refers to the calculation methodology used to achieve RVC 40 that, arithmetically, could be obtained by adding (direct method) the cost of originating materials, labor, overhead, and other expenses or by subtracting (indirect method) from the free on board (FOB) price of the finished good the value of non-originating materials.

The AKFTA wording of *build-up and build down* is inspired by the jargon as contained in the United States (US)–Korea FTA. It is based on the same arithmetical concept of direct and indirect calculations, but there are substantive differences in the calculation methodology.

The direct method used in AANZA, ACFTA, and RCEP is a value-added calculation carrying all the shortcomings of such methodology to calculate the *ad valorem* percentage.[11]

This methodology of calculation is different from the built-up formula used in AKFTA, as in this latter methodology the numerator is represented by the value of originating materials. The AKFTA methodology is thus based on the value of originating materials, and not on a value-added calculation. The built-up calculation is also used in CPTPP and in many other FTAs by US with FTA partners.

By contrast, there is not a marked difference with the *indirect/build down* method as the arithmetical calculation is based on a subtraction of the value of non-originating from the value of the FOB price of the finished product,

Yet there is a difference in the method of calculating the value of non-originating materials among RCEP and AKFTA and other ASEAN+1. RCEP and AKFTA allow the deduction of cost of freight and insurance from the value of non-originating materials. This is a best practice that has progressively emerged in modern FTAs and is especially important for landlocked countries and countries that are not part or are decentralized from logistical hubs. Transport and insurance costs make inputs more expensive for such countries that may be unduly penalized.

---

[10] See Article 2.6 of Regional Comprehensive Economic Partnership Agreement (RCEP). 2020. Legal texts. https://rcepsec.org/legal-text/.

[11] For an assessment of the various calculation methodologies of the *ad valorem*, see Stefano Inama and Pramila Crivelli. 2019. Convergence on the Calculation Methodology for Drafting Rules of Origin in FTAs Using the Ad Valorem Criterion. *Global Trade and Customs Journal.* 14(4): pp. 146–153. https://doi.org/10.54648/gtcj2019014.

Such provision is inserted in paragraph 5 of Article 3.5 of the RCEP:

"5. The following expenses may be deducted from the value of non-originating materials or materials of undetermined origin: (a) the costs of freight, insurance, packing, and other transport-related costs incurred in transporting the goods to the producer; (b) duties, taxes, and customs brokerage fees, other than duties that are waived, refunded, or otherwise recovered; and (c) costs of waste and spillage, less the value of any renewable scrap or by-products. Where the expenses listed in subparagraphs (a) through (c) are unknown or evidence is not available, then no deduction is allowed for those expenses."

Table 3 summarizes the comparative analysis of the architecture and length of the annexes containing PSROs. As noted in previous sections, there has been no effort in standardizing the positioning and length of the annexes containing the protocols on rules of origin among ASEAN+1 FTAs.

This absence of standardization and convergence among ASEAN FTAs is also evident from variations in the level of RVC percentage requirements in the PSROs, which in some ASEAN+1 FTAs, such as AKFTA, varies from 40% to 60% depending on the PSROs; and in the case of AANZA there are sectors where the 35% RVC is required. ACFTA and RCEP maintain a standard RVC, with a 40% requirement.

The length of annexes also varies substantially, with AANZA having the longest, given its approach listing the PSROs at subheading level, while AKFTA and AJCEP are much shorter, as many PSROs are grouped at HS chapter level. Obviously, page number *per se* does not represent a signal of stringency or leniency of the PSROs contained in the various ASEAN+1 FTAs. Yet it is another sign of the heterogeneity of their formulation, with different lengths and details, i.e., HS chapter level, heading or subheading level, positioning of the legal text in the overall protocol of origin, and different percentages. These differences, including changes and updates due to periodic changes in HS nomenclature, are unequivocally complex for firms dealing with such a variety of formulations.

Table 3: Comparing Distribution and Length of PSRO Text among RCEP and ASEAN+1 FTAs

FTA	PRSO Contained in	Length	Rules of Origin Criteria Applied in PSRO	Range of RVC Level
AANZFTA[a]	Annex 2	635 pages[b]	CTC/ CTH/CTSH RVC or CTC/CTH/CTSH WO[c]	Not less than 35% or 40%
ACFTA	Attachment B to Annex 1 of 2019 Amendment[d]	165 pages	WO PE CC/CTH/CTSH RVC Process Rule 1 Process Rule 2 Process Rule 3	Not less than 40%
AJCEP[e]	Annex 2	63 pages 61 pages	CC [f]/CTH/CTSH RVC WO	Not less than 40%
AKFTA[g]	Appendix 2	52 pages (HS2012) 69 pages (HS2017)	CTH/CTSH RVC WO-AK Specific Processes[h]	Mostly not less than 40% or 45% of FOB; sometimes 35%, 55%, 60% of RVC of FOB, respectively. RVC ranges from 45% to 60%
RCEP[i]	Annex 3A	159 pages	RVC CC/CTH/ CTSH WO CR	Not less than 40%

AANZA = ASEAN-Australia New Zealand FTA, ACFTA = ASEAN-People's Republic of China FTA, AJCEPA = ASEAN-Japan Comprehensive Economic Partnership Agreement, AKFTA = ASEAN-Korea Free Trade Agreement, RCEP = Regional Comprehensive Economic Partnership. CC = change of chapter, CR = chemical reaction rule, CTC = change in tariff classification, CTH = change of tariff heading, CTSH = change in tariff subheading, FOB = free on board, PE = produced exclusively from originating materials, RVC = regional value content, WO = wholly obtained, WO-AK = wholly obtained or produced in ASEAN or the Republic of Korea.

[a] See http://aanzfta.asean.org/wp-content/uploads/2016/06/Annex_2_Product_Specific_Rules_1st_Protocol.pdf.

[b] In contrast to other regulations published in A4 Landscape Orientation. Amended 2014; http://aanzfta.asean.org/wp-content/uploads/2016/06/Annex_2_Product_Specific_Rules_1st_Protocol.pdf.

[c] Limited to Chapters 1, 3, 4, 7, 8, 10, 12, and 13.

[d] See https://www.enterprisesg.gov.sg/-/media/esg/files/non-financial-assistance/for-companies/free-trade-agreements/ASEAN-China-FTA/upgrade-protocol/Attachment-B-PSR.pdf.

[e] See http://www.customs.go.jp/roo/english/text/asean2.pdf.

[f] In the case of a good classified under subheadings 1803.10, 1803.20 and 1805.00 of the HS, the total value of non-originating materials used in its production that have not undergone the required CTC does not exceed 10% of the FOB; and in the case of a good classified under subheading 2103.90 of the HS, the total value of non-originating materials used in its production that have not undergone the required CTC does not exceed seven (7)% of the FOB.

[g] See http://www.fta.go.kr/webmodule/_PSD_FTA/asean/1/eng/22.pdf.

[h] Appendix 1, Operational Certification Procedures for the Rules of Origin.

[i] https://rcepsec.org/wp-content/uploads/2020/11/Chapter-3-Annex-3A.pdf.

Source: Authors based on RCEP, AANZA, ACFTA, AJCEP, and AKFTA legal texts.

3. Form of Product-Specific Rules of Origin in RCEP and ASEAN+1 Free Trade Agreements

The form of PSRO is defined as the methodology used to draft PSROs.[12] The form refers to the drafting methodology used to determine the origin of the good, that is, *ad valorem percentage*, change of tariff classification, specific working or processing, or a combination of those.

The substance is, in plain terms, the manufacturing requirement to be carried out in order to comply with the rules of origin.

The form of PSRO also refers to the overall architecture of rules of origin, which can be defined as general (regime-wide) rules of origin and PSROs and, among the latter, those defined at HS chapter, HS heading, or HS subheading levels.

Table 4 compares the distribution of the different specificities of PSROs among the RCEP and ASEAN+1 FTAs, underscoring once again the diversity of approaches used.

On one end of the spectrum, the AANZA revised protocol and RCEP do not provide for general rules, providing only PSROs. AANZA sets PSROs at HS subheading level totaling 5,387 PSROs.

The RCEP follows a similar path to AANZA in the sense that it does not provide for a general rule of origin. Yet the level of detail of RCEP PSROs differs from AANZA, since RCEP sets PSROs at HS chapter level for 33 chapters and 732 PSROs at HS heading level (Table 4).

This explains why the overall number of PSROs of the RCEP is significantly lower than the majority of other ASEAN+1 FTAs.

ACFTA, AJCEP, and AKFTA use a mix of general rules and PSROs.

AJCEP and AKFTA count several PSROs defined at the HS chapter level, heading level, and subheading level, reducing the number of PSROs to 3,568 and 4,667, respectively, in comparison to AANZA, but still significantly higher than the RCEP, with 2,076 PSROs.

Due to its convoluted drafting, the ACFTA stands on its own, since for several HS chapters, ACFTA sets a general CTH rule of origin, while attachment B to Annex 1 of the 2019 ACFTA amendment contains a series of PSROs totalling 2,044.

---

12   For a discussion of the difference of "form" and "substance" of PSROs, see Hoekman and Inama. 2018. Harmonization of Rules of Origin: An Agenda for Plurilateral Cooperation? *East Asian Economic Review*. 22 (1): pp. 3–28. DOI: 10.11644/ KIEP.EAER.2018.22.1.336; and ADB.. 2022. *An Analysis of the Product-Specific Rules of Origin of the Regional Comprehensive Economic Partnership*. http://dx.doi.org/10.22617/TCS220167-2.

Once again, the comparison shows that there is a high diversity of level of specificity of PSROs among the RCEP and ASEAN+1 FTAs. This generates further complexities, as the proliferation of PSROs set at different levels of detail and specificity is a net cost to firms that need to check compliance according to export destination.

The next issue to address is whether this heterogeneity reflects genuine trade interests or is just generated by a different drafting form of the protocol of rules of origin and related PSROs. Section 4 addresses this question.

Table 4: Summary of PSRO Comparisons of ASEAN FTAs and the RCEP

FTA	Number of PSROs at Chapter Level	HS Chapters Covered	Number of PSROs at Heading Level	Number of PSROs at Subheading Level	Number of PSROs under General Rules of Origin	Total PSROs
RCEP	33	1, 2, 6, 10, 14, 26, 33, 36, 37, 42, 45, 49, 57, 58, 59, 60, 61, 62, 65, 66, 67, 68, 69, 73, 82, 86, 88, 89, 92, 93, 94, 95, 97	732	1,311	0	2,076
AANZFTA	0	N/A	0	5,387	0	5,387
ACFTA	N/A	25, 26, 28, 293, 314, 395, 42–49, 57–59, 61, 62, 64, 66–71, 73–83, 86, 88, 91–97	0	2,044	3,343	2,044
AJCEP	18	1,2,3,4,5,6,7,8,10,12,13, 14,41,42,57,58,60,61,64	202	3,348	2,988	3,568
AKFTA	9	1,2,3,5,6,7,10,12,14	136	4,522	3,951	4,667

AANZA = ASEAN-Australia New Zealand FTA, ACFTA = ASEAN-People's Republic of China FTA, AJCEPA = ASEAN-Japan Comprehensive Economic Partnership Agreement, AKFTA = ASEAN-Korea Free Trade Agreement, HS - Harmonized System, PSRO = product-specific rules of origin, RCEP = Regional Comprehensive Economic Partnership.
Source: Compiled by the authors based on analysis of the RCEP, AANZFTA, ACFTA, AJCEP, and AKFTA PSRO.

Table 5 details the use the RCEP and ASEAN+1 FTAs make of the different forms of PSRO. As can be seen in the central column, the use of change of tariff classification in its different forms i.e., CTH or CTSH combined with an alternative RVC, appears to be the most used form of rules of origin across ASEAN+1 FTAs. ASEAN+1 FTAs show peculiar deviations from the common use of CTC or RVC easily detected in Figures 1 to 5.

Table 5: Summary of PSRO Comparison of the RCEP and ATIGA +1 FTAs

| Rule of Origin | No. of PSROs Using Solely RVC | No. of PSROs Using Solely WO | CTC | | | CTC and RVC | | | CTC with Exceptions | | | CTC with alternative requirements | | |
			No. of PSROs using solely CC	No. of PSROs using solely CTH	No. of PSROs using solely CTSH	No. of PSROs using CC and/or RVC	No. of PSROs using CTH and/or RVC	No. of PSROs using CTSH and/or RVC	No. of PSROs using solely WO or CC/CTH or RVC	No. of PSROs using CC/CTH/CTSH with exceptions	No. of PSROs using CC/CTH/CTSH and/or RVC with exceptions	No. of PSROs CC/CTH/CTSH with alternative requirements	No. of PSROs CC/CTH/CTSH and/or RVC with alternative requirements	No. of PSROs using other alternative requirements
RCEP														
HS Chapters	0	2	7	1	0	3	19	0	0	1	0	0	0	0
HS Headings	8	12	141	91	0	30	417	8	0	25	0	0	0	1
HS Subheadings	7	34	120	30	13	96	365	580	0	66	0	0	0	0
Total	**15**	**48**	**268**	**122**	**13**	**129**	**800**	**588**	**0**	**92**	**0**	**0**	**0**	**1**
AANZFTA														
HS Subheadings	77	295	248	107	0	565	2334	1059	45	42	159	109	277	70
Total	**77**	**295**	**248**	**107**	**0**	**565**	**2334**	**1059**	**45**	**42**	**159**	**109**	**277**	**70**
ACFTA														
HS Subheadings	1384	239	352	3	0	212	2578	130	1	25	44	0	235	184
Total	**1384**	**239**	**352**	**3**	**0**	**212**	**2578**	**130**	**1**	**25**	**44**	**0**	**235**	**184**
AJCEP														
HS Chapters	0	0	14	0	0	0	0	0	0	1	0	4	0	0
HS Headings	27	1	48	25	0	19	0	4	0	24	0	54	0	0
HS Subheadings	66	1	96	38	7	7	2,988	26	0	84	16	18	1	0
Total	**241**	**3**	**918**	**149**	**7**	**120**	**2,988**	**41**	**0**	**235**	**16**	**668**	**1**	**0**
AKFTA														
HS Chapters	0	8	0	0	0	0	0	0	0	0	0	0	0	0
HS Headings	2	33	1	1	0	67	1	0	1	0	6	0	24	0
HS Subheadings	67	162	4	0	0	50	3,982	66	4	2	11	0	174	0
Total	**69**	**203**	**5**	**1**	**0**	**117**	**3,983**	**66**	**5**	**2**	**17**	**0**	**198**	**0**

AANZA = ASEAN-Australia New Zealand FTA, ACFTA = ASEAN-People's Republic of China FTA, AJCEPA = ASEAN-Japan Comprehensive Economic Partnership Agreement, AKFTA = ASEAN-Korea Free Trade Agreement, CC = change of chapter, CTC = change in tariff classification, CTH = change of tariff heading, CTSH = change in tariff subheading, FOB = free on board, HS = Harmonized System, PSROs = product-specific rules of origin, RCEP = Regional Comprehensive Economic Partnership, RVC = regional value content, WO = wholly obtained.
Source: Compiled by the authors based on analysis of the RCEP, AANZFTA, ACFTA, AJCEP, and AKFTA PSRO.

Figure 1 of RCEP generally shows a more diffusive spread of different PSRO forms than other ASEAN+1 FTAs. The preponderant use of the CTH or RVC form of PSRO is relevant in the RCEP and in many other ASEAN+1 FTAs, especially for the chemical sectors (HS chapter 29, chemicals). This explains the case for convergence as explained in section 5. Similar to AANZA, the RCEP makes wide use of the CTSH/RVC form of PSRO, especially for chapters 84 and 85 and of the change of chapter (CC) form, especially in the agricultural chapters, where AANZA and AKFTA make extensive use of the wholly obtained form of PSRO.

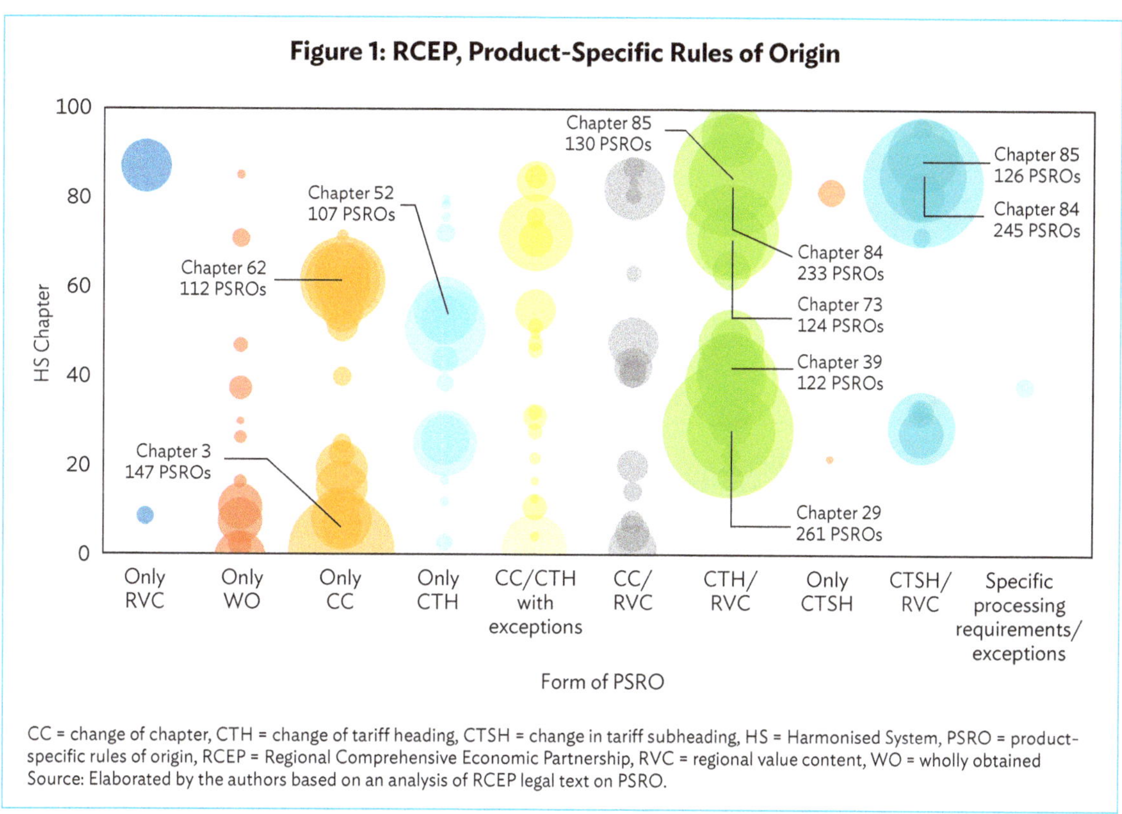

Figure 1: RCEP, Product-Specific Rules of Origin

CC = change of chapter, CTH = change of tariff heading, CTSH = change in tariff subheading, HS = Harmonised System, PSRO = product-specific rules of origin, RCEP = Regional Comprehensive Economic Partnership, RVC = regional value content, WO = wholly obtained
Source: Elaborated by the authors based on an analysis of RCEP legal text on PSRO.

The CC form of PSRO present in the RCEP is spreading to several agricultural chapters also covering textile and clothing sectors. This widespread use of the CC form does not figure into other ASEAN+1 FTAs.

Figure 2 shows AANZA's distinctive preponderant use of the CTSH or RVC 40, compared to other ASEAN+1 FTAs, especially in the chemical and machinery sectors. In other ASEAN+1 FTAs the CTSH/RVC, that is one of most lenient forms of PSRO, is used sparingly, mostly limited to some machinery and electronics in ACFTA, and to even less in AJCEP and AKFTA.

AANZA and ACFTA are similar in the use of CTC with alternative requirements. Notably, this form of PSRO is used in a rather liberal manner in both FTAs. In AANZA, it refers, for instance, to the process of smoking fish in HS chapter 3 or refining oils in HS chapter 15 and, in ACFTA, to the single process rules for textile and clothing.

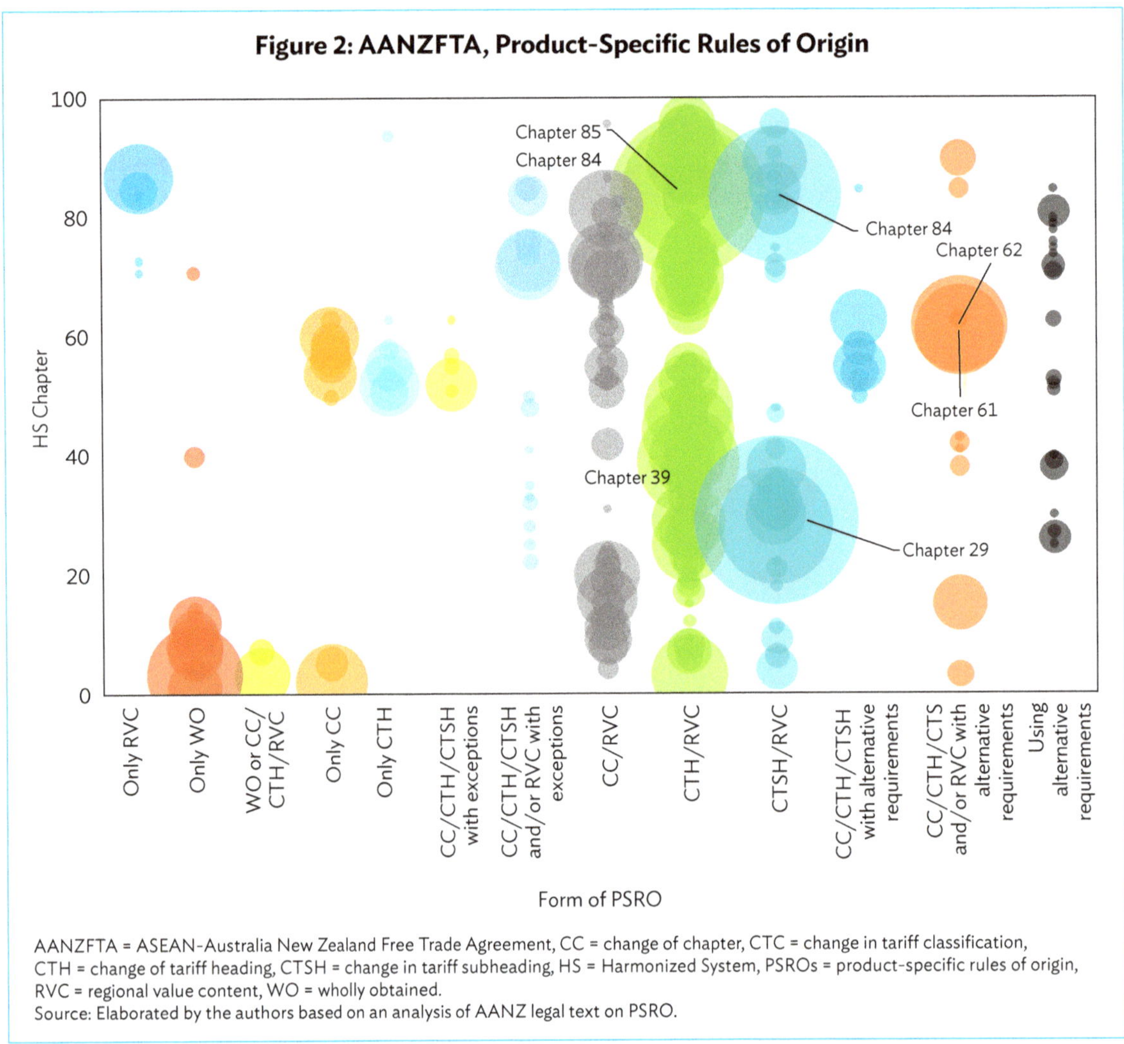

AANZFTA = ASEAN-Australia New Zealand Free Trade Agreement, CC = change of chapter, CTC = change in tariff classification, CTH = change of tariff heading, CTSH = change in tariff subheading, HS = Harmonized System, PSROs = product-specific rules of origin, RVC = regional value content, WO = wholly obtained.
Source: Elaborated by the authors based on an analysis of AANZ legal text on PSRO.

Overall, Figure 2 shows the distinct tendency of AANZA to group PSROs toward the right end of the spectrum, where the most lenient form of PSROs are graphically positioned.

Figure 3 clearly reflects the impact of using two general rules in ACFTA. The distribution of the PSROs is polarized along these two general rules, with RVC 40 spreading in almost all HS chapters, while the CTH/RCV is more concentrated in the processed agricultural products and chemical sectors. There is also a pronounced use of the wholly obtained (WO) and CC form of PSRO in the agricultural chapters, which again shows a tendency to adopt restrictive PSROs in the agricultural chapters. This tendency is also reflected in the RCEP (Figure 1).

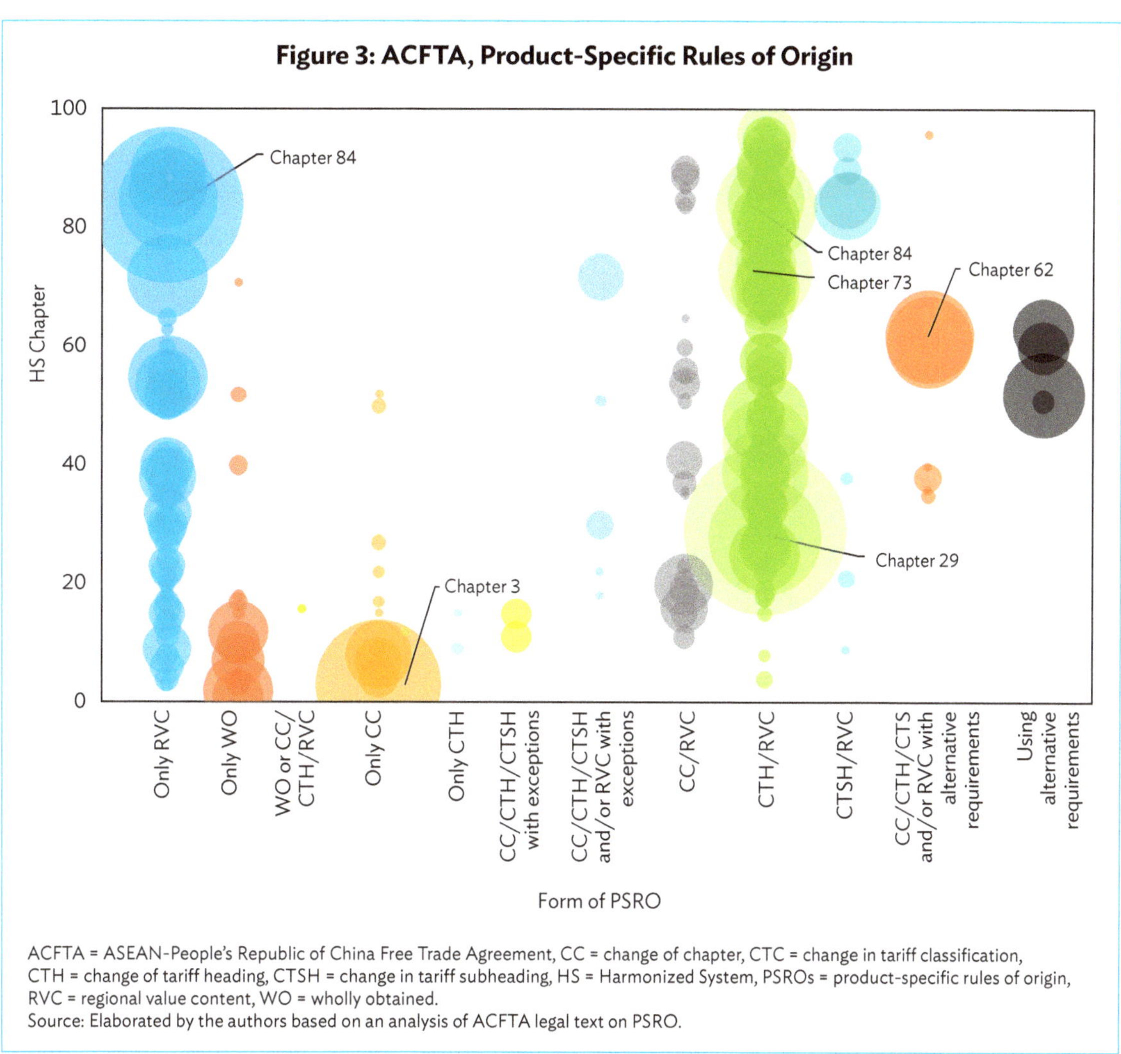

ACFTA = ASEAN-People's Republic of China Free Trade Agreement, CC = change of chapter, CTC = change in tariff classification, CTH = change of tariff heading, CTSH = change in tariff subheading, HS = Harmonized System, PSROs = product-specific rules of origin, RVC = regional value content, WO = wholly obtained.
Source: Elaborated by the authors based on an analysis of ACFTA legal text on PSRO.

Figure 4, depicting the form of PSRO used in AJCEP, clearly shows the absence of the use of the WO form of PSRO, since AJCEP prefers to adopt the CC form for the agricultural chapters. In substantive requirements, there is not a significant difference between the two drafting techniques when used in the first HS agricultural chapters. Conversely, there is an important substantive difference in the way AJCEP uses the CTC method with alternative requirements. AJCEP in fact specifically requires for clothing products of chapter 61 and 62 that, in addition to the CTC with exceptions, the knitting and crocheting or the weaving process of the fabric, as applicable, should be carried out in one of the parties. These PSRO requirements are extremely stringent when compared to the PSROs of other ASEAN+1 FTAs and the RCEP.

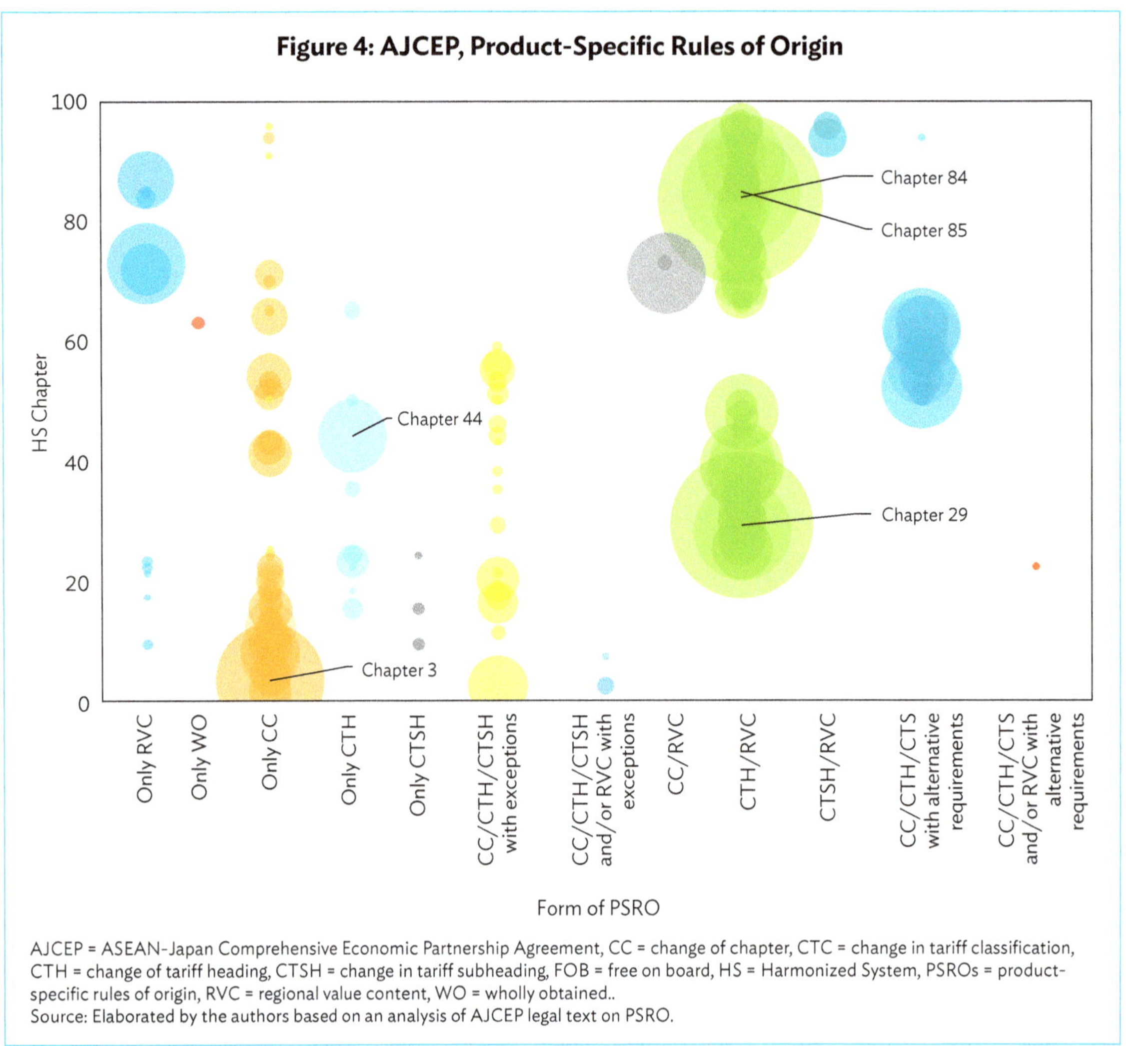

Figure 4: AJCEP, Product-Specific Rules of Origin

AJCEP = ASEAN-Japan Comprehensive Economic Partnership Agreement, CC = change of chapter, CTC = change in tariff classification, CTH = change of tariff heading, CTSH = change in tariff subheading, FOB = free on board, HS = Harmonized System, PSROs = product-specific rules of origin, RVC = regional value content, WO = wholly obtained..
Source: Elaborated by the authors based on an analysis of AJCEP legal text on PSRO.

Figure 5 reflects AKFTA's extensive use of the CTH/RVC as a general rule, as in the case of AJCEP.

AKFTA makes extensive use of the WO form of PSRO for agricultural products, as in the case of other ASEAN+1 FTAs. The use of the CC/RVC form of PSRO is also found in the processed agricultural HS chapters, reflecting the sensitivity of this sector. The use of CTC with alternative requirements is made in a liberal form of PSRO, mostly for textiles and clothing, since it generally provides for CC and the requirements that the good is cut and sewn in the territory of one of the parties or RVC 40. This marks a striking difference from AJCEP.

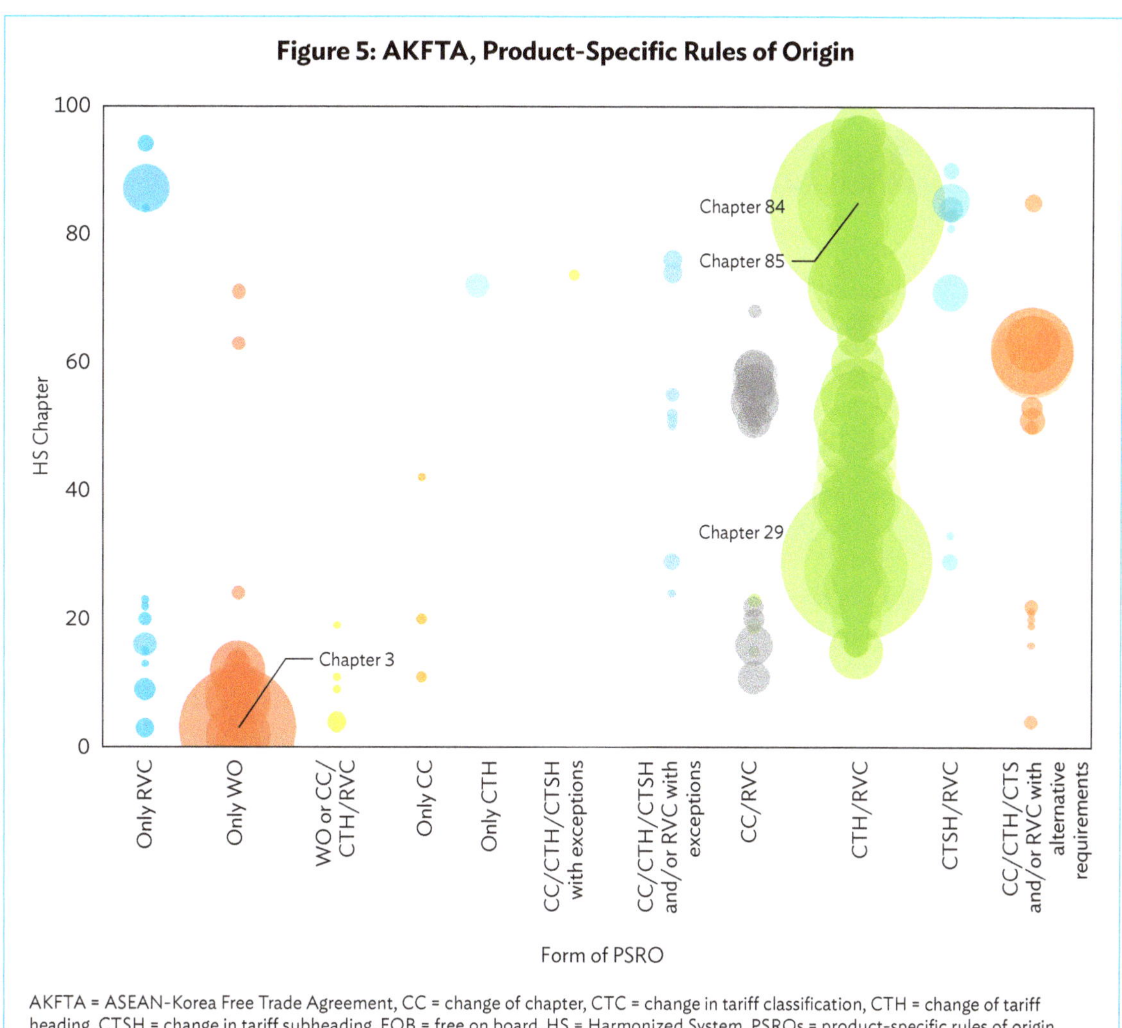

AKFTA = ASEAN-Korea Free Trade Agreement, CC = change of chapter, CTC = change in tariff classification, CTH = change of tariff heading, CTSH = change in tariff subheading, FOB = free on board, HS = Harmonized System, PSROs = product-specific rules of origin, RVC = regional value content, WO = wholly obtained.
Source: Elaborated by the authors based on an analysis of AKFTA legal text on PSRO.

4. Methodology for Assessing Stringency and Leniency of Product-Specific Rules of Origin

The present study utilizes the methodology discussed in previous research.[13] Under this methodology the stringency and leniency of a PSRO may simply refer to "what it takes" to comply with the requirements laid down in PSROs.

As Table 6 shows, a PSRO may be drafted using different forms. Yet, to examine what are the requirements in "manufacturing", it is necessary to spell out for each form of PSRO the different manufacturing requirements to carry out a correct comparison of the leniency and stringency of PSROs contained in the RCEP and ASEAN+1 FTAs.

The PSRO for heading 6101 under RCEP is CC (change of chapter). Since yarns and fabrics to manufacture garments of heading 6101 are classified in other HS chapters, this PSRO allows the use of non-originating yarns and fabrics. In terms of manufacturing requirements, this PSRO means that the cutting, making, and trim of non-originating fabrics into finished garments is an origin conferring operation.

The PSRO requirements under ANZFTA are drafted in a different form since they are set at subheading level and provide for alternative requirements. The first PSRO provides for a RVC of 40% and that the garment is assembled, cut or knit to shape in one of the parties to the FTA, i.e., ASEAN or Australia or New Zealand.

In terms of manufacturing, this first alternative requirement appears stringent with respect to the RCEP, as it requires, in addition to performing the cutting, making, and trim in the territory of one of the parties, an RVC of 40%. The second alternative PSRO providing for a CC is substantially equivalent to the RCEP PSRO.

Thus, the first finding is that, in spite of drafting differences, the respective PSROs under the RCEP and AANZA are equally lenient when using the common CC PSROs. The second finding is that there is scope for convergence, as both FTAs provide for the same PSRO, this being a CC that appears to be the most liberal.

ACFTA provides for 3 alternative rules, namely RVC 40 or CTH or Process Rule 3.

AJCEP provides for a much more complicated drafting using CC, limited by a series of important exceptions to the use of non-originating material classified in different headings, i.e., 52.08 to 52.11, woven fabrics of cotton. This, coupled with the explicit requirement that the weaving has to be carried out in one of the parties means, in terms of manufacturing, a double processing requirement, i.e., weaving of yarn into fabrics and cut, make, and trim operations.

---

[13]   See Stefano Inama. 2022. *Rules of Origin in International Trade* (2nd edition). Cambridge: Cambridge University Press. https://doi.org/10.1017/9781139963206 and ADB. 2022. *An Analysis of the Product-Specific Rules of Origin of the Regional Comprehensive Economic Partnership*. http://dx.doi.org/10.22617/TCS220167-2.

Table 6: Comparison of Product-Specific Rules of Origin for Garments

Product	Product Description	RCEP[a]	AANZFTA[b]	ACFTA[c]	AJCEP[d]	AKFTA[e]
HS 6101	Men's or boys' overcoats, car coats, capes, cloaks … other than those of heading 6103	CC	6101.20; 6101.30; 6101.90: RVC (40) provided that the good is cut or knit to shape and assembled in the territory of one or more of the Parties or CC	6101.20; 6101.30; 6101.90: RVC 40 or CTH or Process Rule 3	CC, provided that, where non originating materials of heading 50.07, 51.11 through 51.13, 52.08 through 52.12, 53.09 through 53.11, 54.07 through 54.08. 55.12 through 55.16 or chapter 60 are used, each of the non-originating materials is knitted or crocheted entirely in one or more of the Parties.	Change to Heading 61.01 from any other Chapter, provided that the good is both cut and sewn in the territory of any Party; or A regional value content of not less than 40% of the FOB value of the good
HS 6201	Men's or boys' overcoats … other than those of heading 6203	CC	**6102.10; 6102.20; 6102.30; 6102.90:** RVC (40) provided that the good is cut or knit to shape and assembled in the territory of one or more of the Parties or CC	**6102.10; 6102.20; 6102.30; 6102.90:** RVC 40 or CTH or Process Rule 3[f]	CC, provided that, where non originating materials of heading 50.07, 51.11 through 51.13, 52.08 through 52.12, 53.09 through 53.11, 54.07 through 54.08, 55.12 through 55.16 or chapter 60 are used, each of the non-originating materials is woven entirely in one or more of the Parties.	Change to Heading 62.01 from any other Chapter, provided that the good is both cut and sewn in the territory of any Party; or A regional value content of not less than 40% of the FOB value of the good

CC = change of chapter, CTC = change in tariff classification, CTH = change of tariff heading, CTSH = change in tariff subheading, FOB = free on board, HS = Harmonized System, RVC = regional value content.

[a] Annex 3A. https://www.enterprisesg.gov.sg/-/media/ESG/Files/Non-Financial-Assistance/For-Companies/Free-Trade-Agreements/RCEP/RCEP_Annex_3A.pdf.

[b] Annex 2. https://www.enterprisesg.gov.sg/-/media/esg/files/Non-Financial-Assistance/For-Companies/Free-Trade-Agreements/ASEAN_Australia_New_Zealand_FTA/Legal_Text/First-Protocol-Appendix-4-Annex-2-Product-Specific-Rules.

[c] Attachment B to Annex 1 of 2019 Amendment https://www.enterprisesg.gov.sg/-/media/esg/files/non-financial-assistance/for-companies/free-trade-agreements/ASEAN-China-FTA/upgrade-protocol/Attachment-B-PSR.pdf.

[d] Annex 2. https://www.enterprisesg.gov.sg/-/media/esg/files/non-financial-assistance/for-companies/free-trade-agreements/ASEAN-Japan-CEP/Legal-Text/Chapter-3/Annex-2-Product-Specific-Rules.

[e] Appendix 2. https://www.enterprisesg.gov.sg/-/media/esg/files/non-financial-assistance/for-companies/free-trade-agreements/ASEAN-korea-fta/AKFTA-PSRs-in-HS-2017-final.pdf.

[f] "Process Rule 3" means manufacturing through the processes of cutting and assembly of parts into a complete article (for apparel and tents) and incorporating embroidery or embellishment or printing (for made-up articles) from: - raw or unbleached fabric; - finished fabric.

Source: Compiled by the authors based on analysis of the RCEP, AANZFTA, ACFTA, AJCEP, and AKFTA PSRO.

Although expressed in a different manner than RCEP and AANZA, AKFTA also provides a CC combined with the requirement that the product is cut and sewn in the territory of a party or an alternative RVC 40. As far as HS 62.01, the same comments are applicable.

This example shows how—beyond the intricacies and the complexity created by the different forms of PSRO used by RCEP and each of ASEAN+1 FTAs,—the degree of leniency is basically the same for RCEP, AANZA, and AKFTA, with AJCEP being more stringent in manufacturing requirements.

This analysis also shows the incredible potential for a simplification of PSROs once the convergence in manufacturing is realized. Once the respective PSROs are unburdened by the technicalities and redundancies, 4 out of 5 of the FTAs provide that cut, make, and trim of non-originating fabrics is origin conferring. Section 5 discusses this further.

5. Methodology for Coding Product-Specific Rules of Origin

PSRO coding has been carried out in similar fashion to the previous ADB study that compared ATIGA, RCEP, and CPTPP rules of origin.

Accordingly, a comparative Microsoft Excel file with all the PSROs of RCEP, AANZA, ACFTA, AJCEP, and AKFTA has been established at the HS six-digits level of disaggregation using the 2012 version. A line-by-line comparison of each HS subheading was carried out on around 27,000 observations based on the manufacturing requirement embedded in the form of the PSROs, as discussed in section 3.

Two kinds of coding have been elaborated. The first one is measuring leniency and stringency of the PSROs of the different FTAs examined with the objective of ranking the FTAs with less stringent PSRO to more stringent PSRO (section 5a).

The second type of coding has been elaborated to measure the convergence among PSROs among the different FTA examined (section 5b).

Coding Stringency

For each HS subheading, PSROs are ranked from the most lenient (code 1) to the most stringent (code 5). Table 7 shows the results of the stringency comparison showing AANZA as the FTA having the least stringent PSROs with 4,300 observations, followed by AKFTA with 3,108.

Notably, AANZA, AKFTA, and RCEP rank at the top. ACFTA ranks fourth and this overall result is mitigated by the convoluted text of the general rules that casts doubts over effective application. AJCEP ranks at the bottom of the ranking with 2,110 lenient PSROs, less than half of AANZA.

In this context, AJCEP also ranks first in having the most stringent PSROs in categories 3, 4, and 5 when compared to other FTAs, making AJCEP the FTA with the most stringent set of PSROs, followed by ACFTA. The overall result of AKFTA having the highest number of category 2 PSROs brings it closer to AANZA and RCEP in overall result, distinct from ACFTA and AJCEP, which clearly tend toward stringency.

In addition, Table 7 shows stringency scores for each FTA. They are calculated by multiplying the number of PSROs with the corresponding number of their stringency level (from 1 to 5). Then, the five scores are added up to obtain the total score, which is shown at the bottom of the table. The last row divides the total score by 5,387, the number of HS subheadings, to obtain an average score corresponding to the average number of HS-heading, weighted by the stringency level. A higher score indicates a higher level of stringency.

Table 7: Stringency Comparison and Scores

Stringency Coding			RCEP	AANZFTA	ACFTA	AJCEP	AKFTA
LEAST STRINGENT	1	No. PSROs	3,053	4,300	2,791	2,110	3.108
		Score (No. PSROs x 1)	3,053	4,300	2,791	2,110	3,108
	2	No. PSROs	1,772	941	1,626	1,831	1,882
		Score (No. PSROs x 2)	3,544	1,882	3,252	3,662	3,764
	3	No. PSROs	525	144	715	841	352
		Score (No. PSROs x 3)	1,575	432	2,145	2,523	1,056
	4	No. PSROs	30	2	243	541	44
		Score (No. PSROs x 4)	120	8	972	2,164	176
	5	No. PSROs	7	0	12	64	1
MOST STRINGENT		Score (No. PSROs x 5)	35	0	60	320	5
Total Stringency Score			**8,327**	**6,734**	**9,920**	**10,779**	**8,109**
Average Stringency Score			**1.55**	**1.25**	**1.84**	**2.00**	**1.51**

AANZFTA = ASEAN-Australia New Zealand Free Trade Agreement, ACFTA = ASEAN-People's Republic of China Free Trade Agreement, AJCEPA = ASEAN-Japan Comprehensive Economic Partnership Agreement, AKFTA = ASEAN-Korea Free Trade Agreement, PSRO = product-specific rules of origin, RCEP = Regional Comprehensive Economic Partnership.
Note: The stringency is represented on a scale of 1 to 5, with 1 being the least stringent and 5 being the most. To find the stringency score, multiply the number of PSROs with the corresponding number of their stringency level (from 1 to 5). For the total stringency, add up all five scores (see last row of the table). For the average score, divide the total score by 5,387, the number of HS subheadings. A lower score indicates less stringency.
Source: Compiled by the authors based on analysis of the RCEP, AANZFTA, ACFTA, AJCEP, and AKFTA PSRO.

Comparing stringency scores strengthens the observation that AANZA is the least stringent agreement, followed by AKFTA, RCEP, ACFTA, and AJCEP. This latter is amply penalized by the 320 PSROs found to be the most stringent compared to all other FTAs examined.

Coding Convergence

In the majority of cases, one or more FTAs present a similar degree of stringency (convergence). More specifically, these PSROs calculated at subheading level are either identical or convergent in terms of manufacturing requirements, as discussed in section 4 above.

The overarching objective of this exercise is to show the potential of convergence as a tremendous trade-facilitating tool to reduce the tangle of overlapping PSROs. To reflect this feature and identify the number of convergent PSROs, the stringency codes have been further disaggregated into "individual" PSRO stringency ("i") or multiple ("x") stringency, as further detailed below:[14]

- If an individual FTA has the least stringent PSRO among the five FTAs, with no other PSRO presenting similar stringency, it takes the value 1i. If two, three or four FTAs have equally stringent PSROs, and if these PSROs are the least stringent compared to the other FTAs, they are each given the value 1x. The FTA(s) with the next most lenient PSRO(s) will be given values of 2i (or 2x).

---

[14] Tables 7 and 8 report the simple stringency count, i.e., the total number of PSROs that have been classified as most lenient (code 1), or ranking 2nd (code 2), 3rd (code 3), 4th (code 4), or most restrictive (code 5), independently of their individual or multiple nature, with S=Si+Sx, where S=[1,2,3,4]).

Box 1: Examples of Stringency Coding

In the case of subheading 0406.10 (Fresh unripened or uncured cheese, including whey cheese, and curd), AANZFTA exhibits the least stringent PSRO among the 5 FTAs, giving the choice between a regional value content (RVC) of 40% or a change of tariff subheading (CTSH).

Therefore, the agreement is assigned the value 1. Both RCEP and ACFTA have been assigned a stringency code of 2x with a RVC of 40%. As the main ingredients of cheese of HS subheading 0406.10 are classified within the same HS chapter 04 (dairy produce; birds' eggs; natural honey; edible products of animal origin) the change of chapter (CC) offered in RCEP as an alternative to RVC of 40% is not more advantageous. As a result, the two PSROs can be viewed as equally stringent, and less lenient than AANZFTA. For the same reason, the CC rule of AJCEP has been codified as the strictest PSRO (3x) among the 5 FTAs, together with the wholly obtained (WO) rule of AKFTA. In both cases, imported ingredients cannot be considered as originating when exporting cheese in partner countries under the FTA, leading to the same stringency codification.

For subheading 1902.11 (Uncooked pasta, not stuffed or otherwise prepared containing eggs), all PSROs based on RVC of 40% are the least stringent. Providing CTH or CC as an alternative to RVC of 40% does not affect the stringency. Eggs and flour are classified in different chapters. Therefore, AANZFTA and ACFTA take the value 1x, and the three other agreements, which only provide CC as a PSRO with no alternative, take the value 2x.

For subheading 1001.11 (Durum wheat seed), the five agreements have either WO or CC as PSROs. Each agreement is assigned the value 1x as all PSROs can be viewed as equally stringent, since CC is not more advantageous than WO due to the raw nature of this agricultural product.

		Product		
HS subheading		0406.10	1902.11	1001.11
HS Description		Fresh unripened or uncured cheese, including whey cheese, and curd	Uncooked pasta, not stuffed or otherwise prepared: containing eggs	Durum wheat seed
RCEP	PSRO	CC or RVC of 40%	CC	WO
	Stringency	2x	2x	1x
AANZFTA	PSRO	RVC of 40% or CTSH	RVC of 40% or CC	WO
	Stringency	1i	1x	1x
ACFTA	PSRO	RVC of 40%	RVC of 40% or CC	WO
	Stringency	2x	1x	1x
AJCEP	PSRO	CC	CC	CC
	Stringency	3x	2x	1x
AKFTA	PSRO	WO	CTH or RVC of 40%	WO
	Stringency	3x	1x	1x

AANZFTA = ASEAN–Australia New Zealand Free Trade Agreement, ACFTA = ASEAN–People's Republic of China Free Trade Agreement, AJCEPA = ASEAN–Japan Comprehensive Economic Partnership Agreement, AKFTA = ASEAN–Korea Free Trade Agreement, CC = change of chapter, CTC = change in tariff classification, CTH = change of tariff heading, CTSH = change in tariff subheading, HS = Harmonized System, PSROs = product-specific rules of origin, RVC = regional value content, WO = wholly obtained. RCEP = Regional Comprehensive Economic Partnership.
Source: Authors based on analysis of the RCEP, AANZFTA, ACFTA, AJCEP, and AKFTA PSRO.

- If an FTA has the second least stringent PSRO, it takes the value 2. If two, three or four FTAs have equally stringent PSROs, and if these PSROs are the second least stringent compared to the other FTAs, they are each given the value 2x.

- If an FTA has the third least stringent PSRO, it takes the value 3. If two or three FTAs have equally stringent PSROs, and if these PSROs are the third least stringent compared to the other FTAs, they are each given the value 3x.

- If an FTA has the fourth least stringent PSRO, it takes the value 4. If two FTAs have equally stringent PSROs, and if these PSROs are the fourth least stringent compared to the other FTAs, they are each given the value 4x.

- If an FTA has the fifth least stringent PSRO, it takes the value 5.

Table 8 reports the results of this disaggregation. The convergence count for each FTA sums the number of PSROs that contain "x", indicating equal stringency to at least one other PSRO. The higher the x count the higher the convergence.

For example, out of the 1,831 PSROs that have been attributed a stringency score of 2 under AJCEP (see simple stringency score in Table 7), 1,582 show equal stringency to at least one other FTA (2x) while 249 are individually ranked as 2nd in terms of stringency, with no other FTA classified in a similar way (no other rank 2).

Results of the convergence count (Table 8, first row) show conspicuous signs of convergence among the different FTAs that are adopting similar or identical PSROs. All FTAs have high values, with the highest in AKFTA (4,830 converging PSROs), showing the scope for a potential simplification exercise of the PSROs.

The findings of this convergence counting, however, should be linked to the stringency codes to realize the scope for convergence and alignment toward the less stringent model of PSRO, as further detailed in the rest of Table 8.

With 3,276 PSROs showing the highest number of convergences with the least stringent PSRO, AANZA could be adopted as a model for convergence, simplification, and trade-facilitating PSROs.

AKFTA and RCEP follow AANZA, recording among the highest number of converging PSROs of the most lenient PSROs according to category 1. These two FTAs also record the first and third highest number of most lenient PSROs in category 2. ACFTA and AJCEP again show potential for aligning themselves to the mainstream to modernize their PSROs according to best practices in AANZA.

Table 8: Convergence and Stringency

STRINGENCY CODING		RCEP	AANZFTA	ACFTA	AJCEP	AKFTA
CONVERGENCE COUNT (SUM)	X	4,352	4,019	3,856	4,055	4,830
LEAST STRINGENT	1i	185	1,024	313	28	217
	1x	2,868	3,276	2,478	2,082	2,891
	2i	500	328	431	249	267
	2x	1,272	613	1,195	1,582	1,615
	3i	322	15	547	474	41
	3x	203	129	168	367	311
	4i	21	1	228	517	31
	4x	9	1	15	24	13
	5	7	0	12	64	1
MOST STRINGENT						

AANZFTA = ASEAN-Australia New Zealand Free Trade Agreement, ACFTA = ASEAN-People's Republic of China Free Trade Agreement, AJCEPA = ASEAN-Japan Comprehensive Economic Partnership Agreement, AKFTA = ASEAN-Korea Free Trade Agreement, RCEP = Regional Comprehensive Economic Partnership.
Note: The stringency is represented on a scale of 1 to 5, with 1 being the least stringent and 5 being the most. The *i* suffix indicates that the PSRO is assigned an individual stringency score (no other FTA has equally stringent PSRO). The *x* suffix indicates the PSROs that are equally stringent in at least 2 FTAs. The convergence count for each FTA sums the number of PSROs that contain "x", indicating equal stringency to at least one other PSRO. The higher the x count the higher the convergence.
Source: Compiled by the authors based on analysis of the RCEP, AANZFTA, ACFTA, AJCEP, and AKFTA PSRO.

To further investigate the convergence of PSRO in different sectors, a methodology to compute a convergence score has been developed. Box 2 shows how the convergence scores are calculated and aggregated at the chapter level. Figure 6 reports the results by HS chapter. The higher the value, the more convergent the chapter's PSROs.

Figure 6 shows that the 5 FTAs are fully convergent in 18 HS chapters. Substantial convergence is also found in the majority of the other HS chapters, with a score of 3 or above, where 4 FTAs out of 5 are converging toward the same degrees of PSRO stringency.

Box 2: How to Calculate the Convergence Scores

The convergence scores (*conv*) can be defined as: *conv=(#x-1)*. Five different general cases can be distinguished for a particular subheading. The different occurrences are reported in the table below.

Full convergence (conv=4)
1. The five FTAs are equally stringent (all codified 1x) or no FTA is individually more stringent or lenient than other FTAs (all codified with "x", no "i").

Partial convergence (conv=[1;3]): one or more FTAs diverge, others converge.

2. One FTA diverges (one "i"), 4 converge (four "x"). The subheading takes the value of three (*conv=3*).
3. Three FTAs show convergence (three "x"). The convergence scores take the value two (*conv=2*).
4. If exactly two among the five FTAs are equally stringent (two "x"), the score is one (conv=1).

Full divergence (conv=0)
5. All individual FTAs present PSROs with different degrees of stringency, the score is zero.

Convergence score	conv=0	conv=1	conv=2	conv=3	conv=4
Dataset cases	1i, 2i, 3i, 4i, 5i	1x, 1x, 2i, 3i, 4i 1i, 2x, 2x, 3i, 4i 1i, 2i, 3x, 3x, 4i 1i, 2i, 3i, 4x, 4x	1x, 1x, 1x, 2i, 3i 1i, 2x, 2x, 2x, 3i 1i, 2i, 3x, 3x, 3x	1i, 2x, 2x, 2x, 2x 1x, 1x, 1x, 1x, 2i 1i, 2x, 2x, 3x, 3x 1x, 1x, 2i, 3x, 3x 1x, 1x, 2x, 2x, 3i	1x, 1x, 1x, 1x, 1x 1x,1x, 2x, 2x, 2x 1x,1x, 1x, 2x, 2x

Note: the codes reflect the value taken by a specific subheading in each of the five agreements.

Chapter average

The score for each chapter is the average score of its subheadings. For example, HS chapter three is composed of a total of 221 subheadings. Each subheading is given a stringency code under each of the five FTAs.

- The five FTAs are equally stringent for 113 of the subheadings (full convergence). These subheadings get the maximum score (four). Their total number of points is 452 (=113 × 4).

- Exactly four out of the five FTAs show convergence for 73 subheadings, with the associated score of three (case 2 above). Their total number of points is 219 (=73 × 3).

- For 35 subheadings, three FTAs are equally stringent, while the remaining two FTAs are either less stringent or more stringent than the group of converging FTAs, but do not have equally stringent PSROs (1x, 1x, 1x, 2i, 3i or 1i, 2x, 2x, 2x, 3i). These subheadings obtain the score of two, with a total number of points of 70 (35× 2).

As a result, the chapter's total number of points is 452 + 219 + 70 = 741. Dividing this value by the number of subheadings (221) yields a final chapter's score of 3.35.

The maximum score for a chapter is 4, indicating the highest degree of convergence. The minimum theoretical score is 0, which indicates no convergence in all subheadings.

Source: Authors.

Figure 6: Convergence by HS Chapter

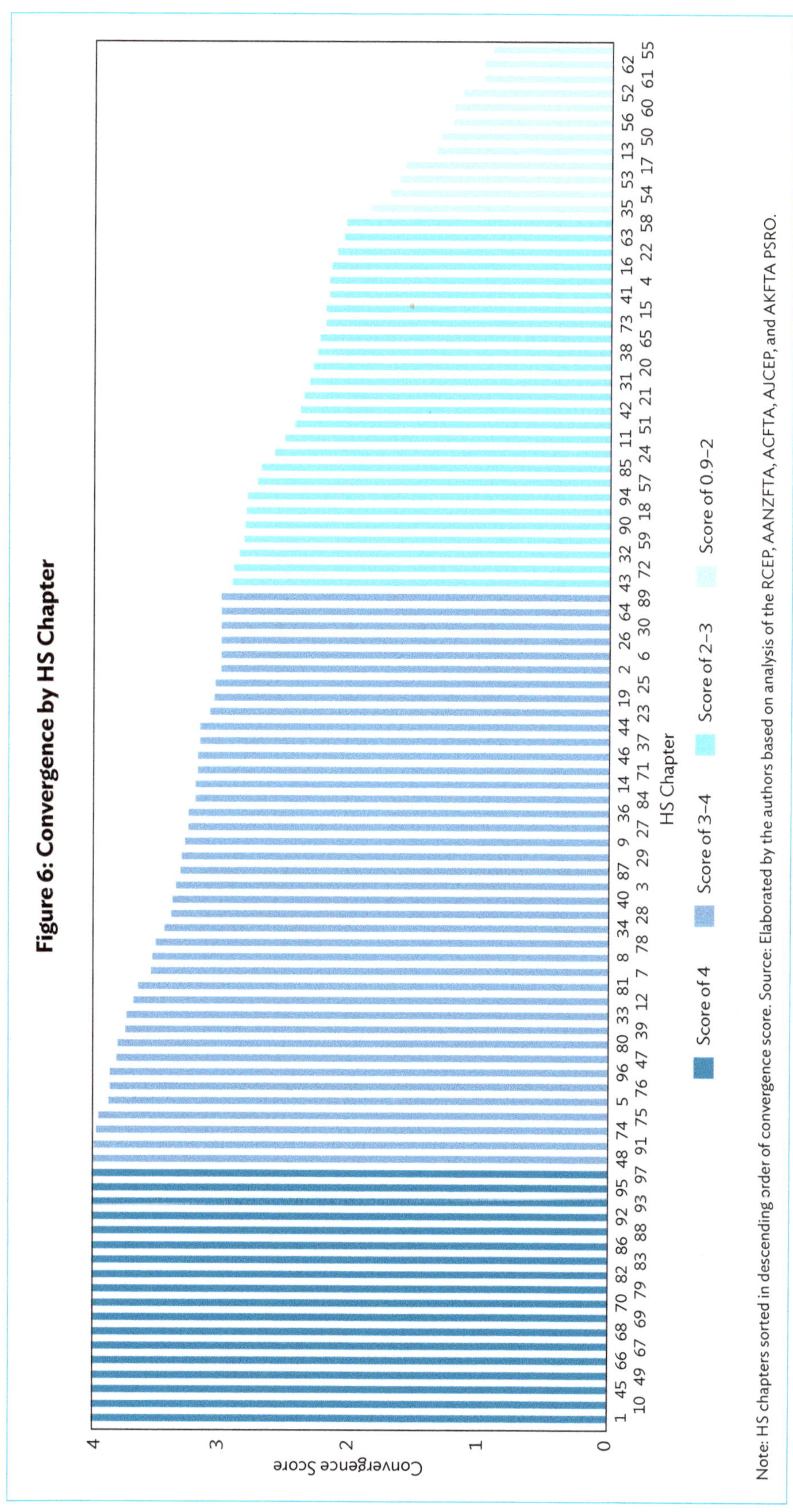

Note: HS chapters sorted in descending order of convergence score. Source: Elaborated by the authors based on analysis of the RCEP, AANZFTA, ACFTA, AJCEP, and AKFTA PSRO.

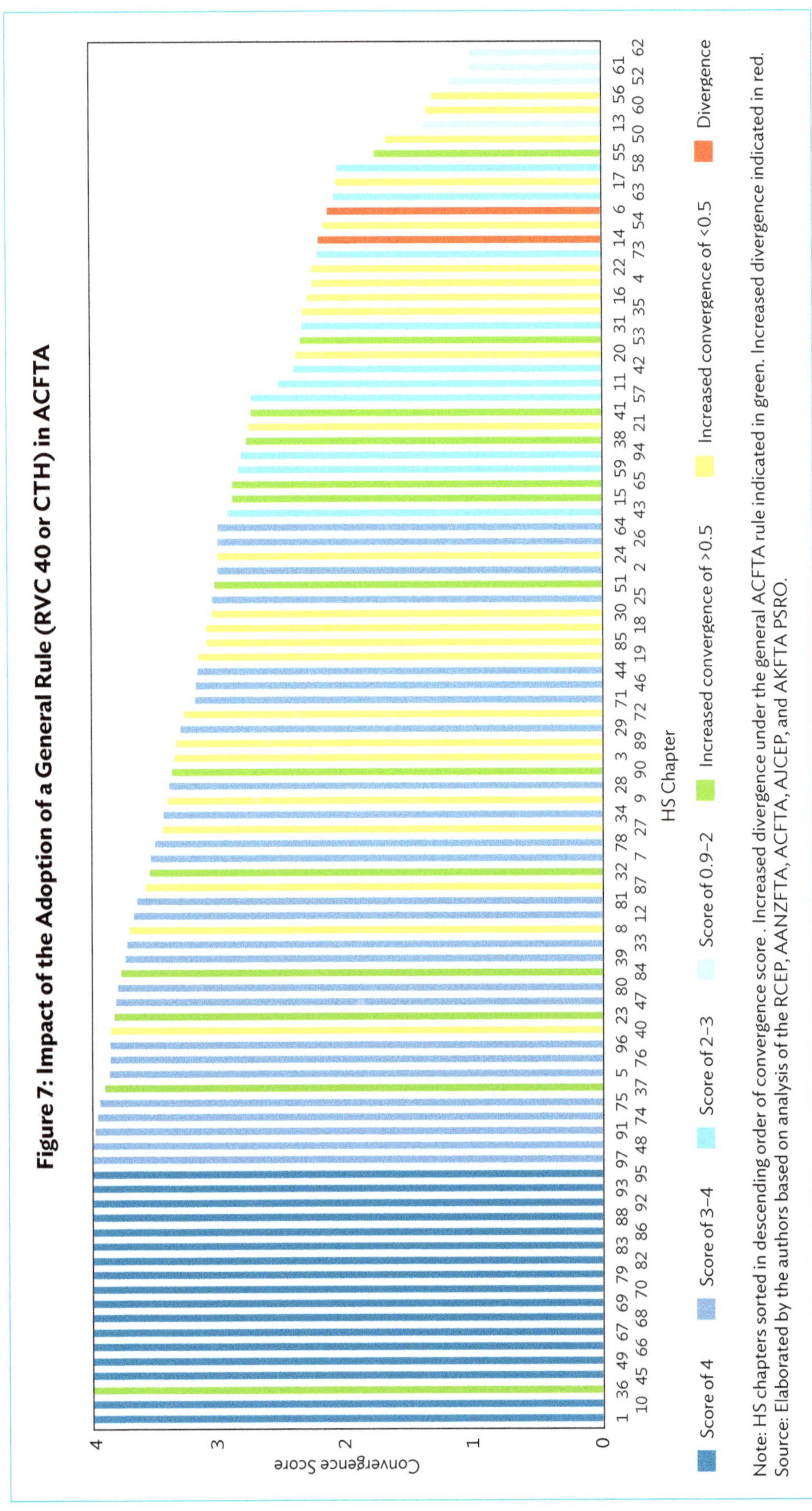

Figure 7: Impact of the Adoption of a General Rule (RVC 40 or CTH) in ACFTA

Note: HS chapters sorted in descending order of convergence score. Increased divergence under the general ACFTA rule indicated in red. Increased convergence of the general ACFTA rule indicated in green. Increased divergence indicated in red.

Source: Elaborated by the authors based on analysis of the RCEP, AANZFTA, ACFTA, AJCEP, and AKFTA PSRO.

Figure 7 shows a similar exercise, simulating that ACFTA adopts a similar general rule of RVC 40 or CTH as adopted by comparable FTAs. Notably, this simple alignment will lead to substantial convergence in a number of HS chapters and increase divergence only on two HS chapters, namely HS chapters 6 and 14.

A simple change in ACFTA's convoluted drafting would bring substantial changes in convergence in key chapters HS 84 and 85, as highlighted in green in Figure 7.

6. Proof of Origin in ASEAN+1 Free Trade Agreements and RCEP

Proof of origin is invariably quoted as one of the most important non-tariff measures by firms. In this area the ASEAN+1 FTAs have not made consistent efforts to streamline the operational certification procedures related to proof of origin.

Thus, in addition to the overlapping proliferation of PSROs generated by the ASEAN+1 FTAs, there has been a parallel growth of different operational certification procedures that, while similar at a distance, are instead painstakingly different among ASEAN+1 FTAs.

The operational certification procedures contained in the RCEP appear to have inherited many complexities existing in ASEAN+1, with no significant progress.

Different methodologies can be used to manage operational certification procedures that could be best summarized as follows:

i. Certificate of origin stamped and signed by certifying authorities (ASEAN+1 FTAs and RCEP)
ii. Certificate of origin signed by exporter (e.g., Canada Generalized System of Preferences)
iii. Statement of origin made by the exporter (e.g., European Union FTAs)
iv. Statement of origin by an approved exporter (e.g., European Union–ASEAN FTAs)
v. Registered exporter (e.g., European Union Generalized System of Preferences and some European Union FTAs)
vi. Importer declaration (mainly US, but also CPTPP and RCEP)
vii. e-certificates of origin (International Chamber of Commerce and other initiatives)
viii. e-certificates of origin via single windows (e.g., ATIGA, 4 ASEAN member states only)

The main difference among the different forms of operational certification procedures relates to the government role in issuing proof of origin and managing operational certification procedures. On one end of the spectrum, the government role is manifested by a certifying authority, commonly customs or the Ministry of Commerce. The certifying authorities are in charge of issuing and certifying certificates of origin based on substantiated requests by exporters. This is the most traditional method of operational certification procedures adopted by ASEAN+1 FTAs.

On the other end, self-certification, either by the exporter or by the importer, has been recently introduced by a number of administrations to facilitate trade transaction and operational certification procedures. For instance, CPTPP adopted the principle of self-certification even with a series of transitional periods for several contracting parties.

While no multilateral rules govern operational certification procedures, except those laid down in annex K of the Kyoto convention, the World Customs Organization Guidelines on Certification of Origin (July 2014, updated in June 2018)[15] and World Trade Organization Nairobi Packagen[16] are setting best practices for encouraging self-certification.

Most recently, ASEAN has embraced electronic certificates of origin exchanged through ASEAN single windows, which have digitalized paper-based certificates of origin and the role of the certifying authority. Yet the role of the authority in validating the information and documentation provided by the exporter remains basically the same.

RCEP adopts the traditional way of operational certification procedures adopted in ASEAN FTAs creating another layer of such procedures and certificates of origin. Yet the RCEP provides for a built-in agenda to progressively move to more trade facilitating practices of operational certification procedures, including self-certification.

Table 9[17] summarizes the main provisions related to issuance of certificates of origin. While a series of ongoing initiatives is introducing less archaic methods of operational certification procedures, the large majority of ASEAN+1 FTAs are still governed by paper-based procedures with exchange of stamps and signatures. This primordial manner of dealing with such procedures is causing many inconveniences in the day-to-day operations and utilization of ASEAN+1 FTAs

---

[15] World Customs Organization (WCO). 2018. Guidelines on Certification of Origin. https://www.wcoomd.org/-/media/wco/public/global/pdf/topics/key-issues/revenue-package/guidelines-on-certification.pdf

[16] World Trade Organization (WTO). 2015. Preferential Rules of Origin for Least Developed Countries. Ministerial Decision of 19 December 2015 : WT/MIN(15)/47 — WT/L/917. https://www.wto.org/english/thewto_e/minist_e/mc10_e/l917_e.htm

[17] The tables are an updated version of United Nations Conference on Trade and Development manual on ASEAN FTA of rules of origin of 2014.

Table 9: Issuance of Certificates of Origin and Notification of Specimen and Stamps in ASEAN+1 FTAs and the RCEP

Agreement	Certificate of Origin Issued by	Information to be Provided
ACFTA	The Certificate of Origin (Form E) shall be issued by the Issuing Authorities of the exporting Party.[a]	Each party shall inform all the other parties of the names and addresses of its respective Issuing Authorities and shall provide specimen signatures and specimen of official seals, and correction stamps, if any, used by its Issuing Authorities. The above information shall be provided by the contact points electronically to all the other Parties to the Agreement through the ASEAN Secretariat, to the extent possible, at least one month before they take effect. A Party shall promptly inform all the other Parties of any changes in names, addresses, or official seals in the same manner.[b] All parties shall promptly provide confirmation that they have received the information to the ASEAN Secretariat, who will forward the compiled confirmation to the submitting party.
AANZFTA	The CO shall be issued by an issuing authority/body of the exporting party. Details of the Issuing authorities/bodies shall be notified by each party, through the ASEAN Secretariat, prior to the entry into force of this agreement. Any subsequent changes shall be promptly notified by each party, through the ASEAN Secretariat.[c]	The issuing authorities/bodies shall provide the names, addresses, specimen signatures and specimens of the impressions of official seals of their respective Issuing authorities/bodies to the other parties, through the ASEAN Secretariat. The Issuing Authorities/Bodies shall submit electronically to the ASEAN Secretariat the above information and specimens for dissemination to the other parties. Any subsequent changes shall be promptly notified through the ASEAN Secretariat. Any CO issued by a person not included in the list may not be honoured by the customs authority of the importing party.[d]
AJCEP	The competent governmental authority of the exporting party shall, upon request made in writing by the exporter or its authorised agent, issue a CO or, under the authorisation given in accordance with the applicable laws and regulations of the exporting Party, may designate other entities or bodies (designees) to issue a CO.[e]	Each party shall provide the other Parties with a list of names and addresses, and a list of specimen signatures and specimen of official seals or impressions of stamps for the issuance of a CO, of its competent governmental authority and, if any, its designees. Any CO bearing a signature not included in the list referred to in paragraph 2 shall not be valid.[f]
AKFTA	Issuing authority means the competent authority designated by the government of the exporting party to issue a CO and notified to all the other parties in accordance with this appendix.[g]	Each party shall provide the names, addresses, specimen signatures and specimen of official seals of its issuing authorities to all the other parties, through the ASEAN Secretariat. Any change in the said list shall be promptly provided in the same manner.[h]

continued on the next page

Table 9 *continued*

Agreement	Certificate of Origin Issued by	Information to be Provided
RCEP	Issuing body means an entity designated or authorised by a party to issue a CO and notified to the other parties in accordance with this chapter.[i]	6: Each Party shall provide the names, addresses, specimen signatures, and impressions of official seals of its issuing body to the other parties. Such information shall be submitted electronically through the RCEP Secretariat established pursuant to subparagraph 1(i) of Article 18.3 (Functions of the RCEP Joint Committee) (RCEP Secretariat), for dissemination to the other parties. Any subsequent changes shall be promptly submitted to the RCEP Secretariat in the same manner for dissemination to the other parties. The parties shall endeavour to establish a secured website to display such information from the last three years, and such website shall be accessible to the Parties. 7: Notwithstanding paragraph 6, a party shall not be required to provide the specimen signatures of its issuing body to the RCEP Secretariat for dissemination to the other parties if it has established its own secured website, containing relevant information of the certificates of origin it issues, including their CO numbers, HS Codes, descriptions of goods, quantities, dates of issuance, and names of the exporters, that is accessible to the parties. The parties shall review the requirement to provide specimen signatures of the issuing bodies three years after the date of entry into force of this agreement for all signatory states.[j]

AANZFTA = ASEAN-Australia New Zealand Free Trade Agreement, ACFTA = ASEAN-People's Republic of China Free Trade Agreement, AJCEPA = ASEAN-Japan Comprehensive Economic Partnership Agreement, AKFTA = ASEAN-Korea Free Trade Agreement, ASEAN = Association of Southeast Asian Nations, CO = certificate of origin, RCEP = Regional Comprehensive Economic Partnership.
[a] ACFTA Annex 1, Attachment A Rule 2.
[b] ACFTA Annex 1 Attachment A Rule 3.
[c] AANZFTA Appendix 2 Section B Rule 1.
[d] AANZFTA Appendix 2 Section B Rule 2.
[e] AJCEP Annex 4 rule 2.
[f] AJCEP Annex 4 rule 2.
[g] AKFTA Appendix 1 Rule 1.
[h] AKFTA Appendix 1 Rule 2.
[i] RCEP Chapter 3 Article 3.1 (i)
[j] RCEP Chapter 3 Article 3.17 para. 6,7.
Source: Authors based on RCEP, AANZA, ACFTA, AJCEP, and AKFTA legal texts.

Table 10 shows the names and format requirements of ASEAN+1 FTAs and the RCEP. Notably, the differences among certificates of origin are not limited to the names of the form and the size of the paper but also to the specific entries of those certificates that are tailored and specific to each ASEAN+1 FTA. In particular, each ASEAN+1 FTA provides lengthy instructions on how to fill the different entries of the certificates of origin.

Each ASEAN + 1 FTA provides specific entries in the certificates of origin to be filled by indicating, for instance, the PSRO complied with, the use of back-to-back certificates of origin or third-party invoicing and other specific entries. Each of these entries are different depending on the ASEAN+1 FTA generating compliance costs and possibly resulting in low utilization.

Table 10: Comparison of Proof of Origin Format and Related Requirements

	AANZFTA[a]	ACFTA[b]	AJCEP[c]	AKFTA[d]	RCEP
Name of the form	Form AANZ	Form E	Form AJ	Form AK	Certificate of Origin; or Declaration of Origin (i.e., self-declaration) as an approved exporter, or as an exporter or producer of the goods in question[e,f]
Specimen	Attachment of AANZFTA Minimum data requirements in Appendix 2	Annex 1, attachment C: Certificate of Origin Form E Revised	Attachment to Annex 4 of AJCEP, revised version published 2014	Attachment of Annex 3, Appendix 1	Chapter 3, Section B: Operational Certification Procedures
Format	Hardcopy; in English	ISO A4 size white paper; in English	In English, A4 size paper,	A4 paper; in English	In writing, or any other medium, including electronic format as notified by an importing Party; in English; specify that the good is originating and meets the requirements of this Chapter (Chapter 3); contains information which meets the minimum information requirements as set out in Annex 3B (Minimum Information Requirements)[g] CO: in format to be determined by the Parties; bear a unique CO number; in English; bear an authorised signature and official seal (applied manually or electronically) of the issuing body of the exporting party[h] *Declaration of Origin*: in English, bear the name and signature of the certifying person; bear the date on which the Declaration of Origin was completed[i]

continued on the next page

Table 10 *continued*

	AANZFTA[a]	ACFTA[b]	AJCEP[c]	AKFTA[d]	RCEP
Copies	1 original; 2 copies	1 original; 2 copies	In the case of a Party which is an ASEAN Member State: 1 original, 2 copies In the case of Japan: original only	1 original; 2 copies The colours of the original and the copies shall be mutually agreed upon by the parties.	1 original; certified true copy (in case of theft, loss, or destruction of an original CO)
Distribution of copies	Original be forwarded by exporter to importer for submission to the customs authority of the importing party. Duplicate retained by the issuing authority. Triplicate retained by the exporter.	Original forwarded, by exporter to importer for submission to the customs authority Duplicate retained by issuing authority. Triplicate retained by exporter.	Original forwarded by the exporter to importer for submission to customs authority of importing Party. In the case of a Party which is an ASEAN Member State, a copy of the CO is to be retained by both the exporter and the competent governmental authority of the exporting party or its designees, respectively.	Original forwarded by the producer and/or exporter to importer for submission to the customs authority of the importing party. The duplicate retained by issuing authority of the exporting Party. The triplicate retained by producer and/or exporter.	

AANZFTA = ASEAN-Australia New Zealand Free Trade Agreement, ACFTA = ASEAN-People's Republic of China Free Trade Agreement, AJCEPA = ASEAN-Japan Comprehensive Economic Partnership Agreement, AKFTA = ASEAN-Korea Free Trade Agreement, ASEAN+1 FTA = Association of Southeast Asian Nation plus-1 Free Trade Agreement, ATIGA = ASEAN Trade in Goods Agreement, CO = certificate of origin, CPTPP = Comprehensive and Progressive Agreement for Trans-Pacific Partnership, RCEP = Regional Comprehensive Economic Partnership.

a   Appendix 2, http://aanzfta.asean.org/wp-content/uploads/2017/02/AANZFTA-First-Protocol-Appendix-2B2.pdf.
b   http://www.asean.org/storage/images/archive/documents/acfta/Appendix1-101125.pdf.
c   http://www.mofa.go.jp/policy/economy/fta/asean/implement.pdf.
d   Appendix, http://akfta.asean.org/uploads/docs/akfta-operational-certification-procedures.pdf.
e   The parties shall commence a review of this Article on the date of entry into force of this Agreement for all signatory States. This review will consider the introduction of declaration of origin by an importer as a proof of origin. The parties shall conclude the review within five years of the date of its commencement, unless the Parties agree otherwise. Notwithstanding this paragraph, Japan may, from the date of the entry into force of this agreement for it, consider a Declaration of Origin by an importer as a Proof of Origin in the same manner as Proof of Origin under paragraph 1 (Art. 3.16).
f   Australia, Brunei Darussalam, People's Republic of China, Indonesia, Japan, Republic of Korea, Malaysia, New Zealand, Philippines, Singapore, Thailand, and Viet Nam shall implement subparagraph 1(c) (Declaration of Origin by an exporter or producer) no later than 10 years after their respective dates of entry into force of this Agreement. Cambodia, Lao PDR, and Myanmar shall implement subparagraph 1(c) no later than 20 years after their respective dates of entry into force of this agreement.
g   Chapter 3, Section B, Article 3.16, 5(a).
h   Chapter 3, Section B, Article 3.17, 3.
i   Chapter 3, Section B, Article 3.18, 2.

As reported from recent analysis of the status of the implementation of ATIGA, the incorrect filling of certificate of origin entries may result in denial of preferential treatment at customs clearance. Analysis of the results of the debates in the ATIGA ad hoc committee shows that even the use of wrong ink (black or blue) in ticking the boxes of the entry may generate difficulties in the application of preferential treatment. The same occurrences may take place during implementation of ASEAN+1 FTAs, since the format of the certificates of origin and related operational certification procedures are largely similar.

Recent studies[18] have linked the combined heterogeneity of PSRO and operational certification procedures as one of the main reasons for low utilization of ATIGA trade preferences.

Such analysis has shown that in 2016–2018, average utilization rates of ATIGA have been 50%, even after introduction of electronic certificates of origin following the ASEAN single window initiative.

Table 11 in fact shows an increase in utilization rates from a low of 43.5% in 2016 to 57.6% in 2018.

Table 11: ATIGA Utilization Rates by Year

	2016	2017	2018
Average ASEAN Utilization Rates	43.5%	51.3%	57.6%

ATIGA = ASEAN Trade in Goods Agreement.
Source: Inama, Crivelli, and Ha (2022) based on ASEAN Secretariat data.

In spite of the relative improvement in 2018, the utilization rates of ATIGA may be considered low, especially for an FTA that has been in force for almost a decade. In comparison, the LD utilization rates of trade preferences granted to least developed countries by the Quadrilateral group of Canada, the European Union, Japan, and the US was 90% in 2018.

Calculations have shown that the amount of possible duty savings for ASEAN firms was $3.6 billion in 2018. Duty savings are those duties that could have been saved if trade preferences were fully utilized.

The ASEAN Free Trade Area, ATIGA PSROs, and operational certification procedures have been through various iterations and negotiations in the last decades, to no avail. A document emerging[19] from the ASEAN intergovernmental machinery shows that from 2008 to 2021, not less than 36 intergovernmental meetings were held. with 89 issues raised over the difficulties and misunderstandings of ATIGA application of rules of origin.

---

18   See Stefano Inama, Pramila Crivelli, and Phan Manh Ha. 2022. The Low Use by Firms of ASEAN Trade Preferences: Will RCEP Follow the Same Destiny? An Agenda for Rescue to Reform Rules of Origin in the Asian and Pacific Region. *Global Trade and Customs Journal*. 17(6). pp. 248–251. https://doi.org/10.54648/gtcj2022033.

19   Excerpt from the Sub-Committee on ATIGA Rules of Origin meeting of 21–23 June 2021.

7. Conclusion and Recommendations

This study highlights the need to simplify the tangle of PSROs and operational certification procedures in FTAs in Asia and the Pacific. The detailed analysis contained in the first ADB study (footnote 8) estimating the incremental value of RCEP rules of origin over those contained in ATIGA and the CPTPP already revealed the limitation of RCEP rules of origin. Yet, experts, policy makers, and observers stressed the need to complete the analysis with a "fairer" comparison of the RCEP with the ASEAN+1 FTAs that are directly competing with the RCEP and share common institutional history, background, and negotiating processes. As the RCEP was conceived with the idea to expand, deepen, and simplify the negotiations with dialogue partners, it was expected that a comparison with ASEAN+1 FTAs would reveal the potential of RCEP in addressing the "noodle bowl" of overlapping PSROs and operational certification procedures in the region.

The analysis shows that RCEP scores better in leniency of PSROs than the oldest ASEAN+1 FTAs, such as ACFTA and AJCEP. However, it does not show better results than AANZA PSROs, reviewed in 2015. Overall, the analysis failed to demonstrate that RCEP PSROs and operational certification procedures do provide significant, incremental value over existing ASEAN+1 FTAs. Perhaps due to the multiplicity of countries involved in the negotiations, the RCEP does not set a new standard or best practices on PSROs and operational certification procedures. Leveraging on the "built-in" agenda, further negotiations could be pursued to unlock the potential of the RCEP in boosting intra-regional trade, with business-friendly PSROs and operational certification procedures that will provide effective incentives to firms in Asia and the Pacific to use the RCEP instead of the older ASEAN+1 FTAs.

This study also shows that the PSROs of ACFTA and AJCEP are old and stringent compared to advances in AANZA and the RCEP. In particular, the drafting of the ACFTA protocol on rules of origin and the main general rules shows lack of clarity and transparency, generating difficulties during implementation. Redressing such flaws would require strong commitment by ASEAN members and coordinated action by its intergovernmental institutional machinery. The research findings provide insights on where to start the process. Similar to the first ADB study comparing RCEP with CPTPP and ATIGA, this comparative analysis has found significant scope for convergence and simplification of PSROs and operational certification procedures among RCEP and ASEAN+1 FTAs.

The results of the coding exercise suggest sectors and HS chapters where the RCEP and ASEAN+1 PSROs could be substantially reviewed towards greater convergence and simplification, indicating where (i) PSROs could be made more lenient, and (ii) PSROs are converging across RCEP and ASEAN+1 FTAs.

The results of the coding exercise and comparative analysis highlight the conspicuous number of PSROs where the RCEP and ASEAN+1 FTAs converge to identical or similar rules. As demonstrated in the earlier study, the same findings are valid for the RCEP, ATIGA, and the CPTPP. This research also shows areas of divergence, but those are relatively minimal in comparison to areas of convergence. These findings suggest that the case for harmonizing existing rules of origin in RCEP, ATIGA, and ASEAN+1 FTAs is stronger than ever.

For companies to benefit from the opportunities provided by the RCEP, further steps are needed to turn this analysis into an actionable document that could be discussed at the intergovernmental level, using for instance the RCEP built-in agenda.

The first step would be to use the results about the convergence and leniency in both studies to identify the main HS chapters among the seven FTAs that have shown convergence and leniency. These results could be grouped into a template and officially submitted for discussion during forthcoming intergovernmental meetings under the ASEAN/RCEP agenda. The template could clearly indicate that, where possible, one single PSRO across FTAs should be used. Where such convergence is not possible, because for instance a party wishes to maintain CC instead of WO in HS chapter 1, that option would be maintained. This consolidation in two possible forms of convergence would nevertheless already significantly contribute to enhance simplicity and transparency while lowering compliance costs.

Similar exercises could be repeated for those HS chapters where partial convergence among the seven FTAs is observed, highlighting the different variations and where possible, showing options for further convergence. In fact, the results of both studies show that, in many cases, different and divergent PSROs are not the result of a reasoned trade interest but are sometimes adopted by default or based on political economy determinants (Crivelli, Inama, and Marand 2023) or other non-economic reasoning. In those cases, a simple scrutiny exercise will surely trigger additional convergence and trade facilitation.

The template should record areas or HS chapters where divergence is observed, and report the different options. Even in this area, simple consolidation efforts showing where divergence exists create awareness among governments and firms, reducing compliance costs and facilitating consultations.

Similar research is needed to identify the best practices and lessons learned in the area of operational certification procedures. The latter has shown to be a significant non-tariff measure and a hurdle for Asian and Pacific firms to comply with to fully utilize ATIGA. Most likely, similar hurdles are encountered by firms wishing to use ASEAN+1 FTAs since, as examined in section 6 of this paper, ASEAN+1 operational certification procedures share many of ATIGA's peculiarities and complexities.

Asia and the Pacific, and especially ATIGA, has a history of arguably complexity about operational certification procedures as discussed in section 6. Reducing such complexities would help address the problem of low utilization of FTAs in the region (see Inama, Crivelli, and Ha 2022).

The region has vigorously embarked on information technology solutions to manage operational certification procedures related to origin (e.g., e-certificate of origin), trying to address inefficiencies and red tape. At the same time, some Asian and Pacific countries are moving to self-certification, together with major trading nations in the western hemisphere, as recommended by the World Customs Organization Guidelines for operational certification procedures promoting self-certification as best practice. Given the different approaches, research and surveys need to be carried out in the region to identify the lessons on operational certification procedures relying on information technology solutions and explore ways to combine those with self-certification procedures for better efficiency and authenticity verification.

References

Asian Development Bank. 2022. *An Analysis of the Product-Specific Rules of Origin of the Regional Comprehensive Economic Partnership.* Manila: Asian Development Bank. http://dx.doi.org/10.22617/TCS220167-2.

Association of Southeast Asian Nations (ASEAN). 2021. *Decisions of SC-AROO, ROOTF, CCCA, AFTA Council on Implementation Issues.* https://asean.org/wp-content/uploads/2021/09/Matrix-of-ROO-Implementation-Issues-16-Aug-2021-1.pdf.

ASEAN-Australia-New Zealand Free Trade Agreement (AANZA). 2015. Legal texts. https://aanzfta.asean.org/agreement-establishing-the-aanzfta.

ASEAN-People's Republic of China Free Trade Agreement (ACFTA). 2019. Legal texts. https://www.enterprisesg.gov.sg/-/media/esg/files/non-financial-assistance/for-companies/free-trade-agreements/acfta/acfta_legal_text.pdf.

ASEAN-Japan Comprehensive Economic Partnership (AJCEP). 2022. Legal texts. https://www.mofa.go.jp/policy/economy/fta/asean.html.

ASEAN-Republic of Korea Free Trade Agreement (AKFTA). 2015. Legal texts. https://akfta.asean.org/index.php?page=agreement.

Crivelli, P. and S. Inama. 2021. Making RCEP Successful Through Business-friendly Rules of Origin. Asian Development Blog. Manila. https://blogs.adb.org/blog/making-rcep-successful-through-business-friendly-rules-origin.

Crivelli, P. and S. Inama. 2022. A Preliminary Assessment of the Regional Comprehensive Economic Partnership. *ADB Briefs.* No. 206. Manila: Asian Development Bank. http://dx.doi.org/10.22617/BRF220009-2.

Crivelli, P., S. Inama, and J. Marand. 2023. The Determinants of Product-Specific Rules of Origin: An Econometric Analysis in the Regional Comprehensive Economic Partnership. ADB Economics Working Paper. Forthcoming. Manila: Asian Development Bank.

Inama, S. 2022. *Rules of Origin in International Trade* (2nd edition). Cambridge: Cambridge University Press. https://doi.org/10.1017/9781139963206.

Inama, S. and P. Crivelli. 2019. Convergence on the Calculation Methodology for Drafting Rules of Origin in FTAs Using the Ad Valorem Criterion. *Global Trade and Customs Journal.* 14(4): pp. 146–153. https://doi.org/10.54648/gtcj2019014.

Inama, S. and E.W. Sim. 2015. Rules of Origin in ASEAN: A Way Forward (Integration through Law: The Role of Law and the Rule of Law in ASEAN Integration) (Vol. 1). Cambridge: Cambridge University Press. https://doi.org/10.1017/CBO9781316145128.

Inama, S., P. Crivelli, and P.M. Ha. 2022. The Low Use by Firms of ASEAN Trade Preferences: Will RCEP Follow the Same Destiny? An Agenda for Rescue to Reform Rules of Origin in the Asian and Pacific Region. *Global Trade and Customs Journal.* 17(6). pp. 248–251. https://doi.org/10.54648/gtcj2022033.

Hoekman, B. and S. Inama. 2018. Harmonization of Rules of Origin: An Agenda for Plurilateral Cooperation? *East Asian Economic Review*. 22 (1). pp. 3–28. March. https://dx.doi.org/10.11644/KIEP.EAER.2018.22.1.336.

Regional Comprehensive Economic Partnership Agreement (RCEP). 2020. Legal texts. https://rcepsec.org/legal-text/.

World Customs Organization (WCO). 2018. Guidelines on Certification of Origin. https://www.wcoomd.org/-/media/wco/public/global/pdf/topics/key-issues/revenue-package/guidelines-on-certification.pdf.

World Trade Organization (WTO). 2015. Preferential Rules of Origin for Least Developed Countries. Ministerial Decision of 19 December 2015: WT/MIN(15)/47 — WT/L/917. https://www.wto.org/english/thewto_e/minist_e/mc10_e/l917_e.htm.